A
NEW
GEOGRAPHY
OF
POETS

A NEW GEOGRAPHY OF POETS

COMPILED AND EDITED BY
EDWARD FIELD
GERALD LOCKLIN
CHARLES STETLER

The University of Arkansas Press / Fayetteville / 1992

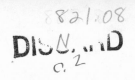

Copyright 1992 by Edward Field, Gerald Locklin, and Charles Stetler
All rights reserved
Manufactured in the United States of America
96 95 94 93   5 4 3 2

This book was designed by Chiquita Babb using the New Baskerville and Lithos typefaces.

The paper used in this publication meets the minimum requirements of the American National Standard for Permanence of Paper for Printed Library Materials Z39.48-1984. ∞

Library of Congress Cataloging-in-Publication Data

A new geography of poets / compiled and edited by Edward Field, Gerald
    Locklin, Charles Stetler.
        p. cm.
    Includes index.
    ISBN 1-55728-240-4. — ISBN 1-55728-241-2 (pbk.)
        1. American poetry—20th century. 2. United States—Poetry.
    I. Field, Edward, 1924–   . II. Locklin, Gerald. III. Stetler, Charles.
PS615.N39 1992
811'.5408—dc20   91-46003
                                                            CIP

There always was a relationship between poet and place. Placeless poetry, existing in the non-geography of ideas, is a modern invention and not a very fortunate one.

—Archibald MacLeish

CONTENTS

CONTENTS

THE NORTHEAST

THE OLD WEST

SOUTHERN CALIFORNIA

INTRODUCTION

A New Geography of Poets—where the poets are. An anthology that sets out to demonstrate that poets—good poets—are to be found, not just in a few cities and cultural centers but everywhere in America. We can't include all of them, of course, and have even left out many of the most famous. But in this selection we set out to give the reader a pretty fair map of poetry at the beginning of the nineties.

Beyond locating America's poets, we ask, What do they say about where they are? This volume contains some of the answers, with poems that explore the world the poets live in. However, it is not our interest to settle for mere landscape poetry but to choose poems that reveal the spirit of the place and of the poet, aiming for a balance between inner and outer geography.

For the "geography" of poets is not only where they happen to be. Along with the news of the world around them, their poems report the state of the world inside: the cities and highways, rivers and mountains, yes, who and what populates the landscape—human, vegetable, and animal—but also the poets' inner geography, where ancestors, old neighborhoods, and political issues mingle.

In our geography are poets of a rainbow of backgrounds, of a post–melting-pot consciousness:

> There always was that menu
> that was in Spanish
> that reassured us that
> this was a good place. . . .
>> ("Burrito," by Raphael Zepeda)

Where they, their parents, and their parents' parents come from is a vital clue in locating "where the poets are." In "West Indian Primer," Elizabeth Alexander, of Philadelphia, tells what she knows about her roots:

> "On the road between Spanish-Town
> and Kingston," my grandfather said,
> "I was born" . . .

In the outer landscape the geography of poets includes the workplace:

> They walk around with big sheets of sheet metal,
> bending and buckling them
> until they whirr and hum
> ("Lingo," by Fred Voss)

the railroads:

> The Erie-Lackawanna trains are the ghosts
> of summer nights . . .
> ("Note in a Bottle," by Gerald McCarthy)

and the racetrack:

> at the racetrack I sit in my clubhouse seat
> smoking cigarette after cigarette
> (*from* "Horsemeat," by Charles Bukowski)

For most of us, movie stars and celebrities also loom large in our inner landscapes. Joan Jobe Smith, growing up in Long Beach, remembers her adolescence when

> Robert Wagner began peeking into my
> bedroom window on nights the moon was full.
> ("Heartthrobs")

Anselm Hollo of Utah even defines the special geography of the

> . . . life of the artists
> in the land of art.
> ("In the Land of Art")

The geography of our poets goes even further than the geographical limits of America itself, for poets are hardy travelers, translators of foreign poets, as well as fantasizers of other worlds.

When *A Geography of Poets* came out in 1979, a top New York editor declared point blank, "This is an anti-New York anthology." That of course was a negative interpretation of what I was trying to do, which was to show what was going on in the poetry scene in other parts of the country and, for once, to give equal space to it. But his reaction gives some indication of the politics of poetry, and the control over poetry exerted from the power center of the publishing world, that we, the editors, with this volume are trying to correct. For without attacking New York City (which in many ways is the most liberal and intellectual city in the country), we continue to feel it unhealthy and undesirable that poetry should be mediated and judged by the special, mandarin values of such a limited circle, that the rest of American poetry should be filtered through a set of standards inappropriate, and perhaps inimical, to it—especially when the populist traditions in American poetry are for the most part ignored by the elitists of Northeast academic criticism.

The issue of Highbrow vs. Lowbrow seems to lie at the heart of the controversy. Highbrow in the power circles of the Northeast, proclaimed by critics like Harold Bloom and Helen Vendler, is very much "in." But in much of the rest of the country, Lowbrow is triumphant, and vernacular poetry growing out of populist sentiments has exploded with a compelling verve and energy. The National Endowment for the Arts, though currently threatened by controversy, has spread grant money around the country and encouraged and ennabled poets of all schools, especially ethnics, to go on writing. It is the small presses and university presses that have responded to the growing numbers of poets, while the large publishers in New York and Boston, now owned by multi-national corporations, have been cutting down their lists.

The first *Geography* presented what the editor hoped was an un-parochial view of American poetry. This had to do with poetry that spoke in recognizably human voices, often the voices of our various minority populations (that together almost make up the majority today), using the vernacular language, and about subjects that mattered. His idea was that poetry, even that of the most formal poets, should be as interesting, if not always as easy, to read as the newspaper, embody the idealism of the poetic impulse, and have a content that related to real life, both tragic, caustic, and funny. In this, the editors of this volume concur.

Though the poems in the first *Geography* were not chosen for geographical pertinence, the poetry of the different areas of the country did seem to have something of their own "flavor." With the *New Geography*, beyond presenting the best of the poetry actually coming out of the different geographical regions, we have decided to take the theme of "geography" literally—to find poetry that in some way reflects the geography of the title, specifically relating to the region. But we are not trying to define what is a southern poet, for example, or a New York poet. Every area of the country has experienced an "invasion" of poets from elsewhere. Though a number of local poets remain who demonstrate what are considered to be regional characteristics, poets move around as much as, if not more than, everyone else in the country, and they have settled down everywhere, no matter where they were born, bringing their backgrounds, and different ideas about poetry, with them. So we have included in the South, for example, poets who are not "southern," but merely live there, choosing the poem or poems that give evidence that where they live has affected them in some way.

The Northwest region, with a still-recent frontier tradition and remnants of wilderness, as well as its proximity to the Far East, has been dominated by a wide range of cult concerns—New Age, ecology, Pacific Rim consciousness, Buddhism, Indian lore, and the various liberation movements. Despite traditional American attitudes to poetry as "sissy" or the province of women, poetry in the Northwest is almost a macho tradition, allied to outdoor activities like logging and fishing and, in a popular fantasy of being possessed by the returning souls of Indians, living off the land. Jana Harris writes out of her experiences on fishing boats in Alaska:

> We fish our lives out,
> drink
> crash
> wake up
> leave at 6, drink
> fish till dark
> ("We Fish Our Lives Out")

Besides the San Francisco Bay Area, throughout the Northwest exist centers of poets, in Bolinas (California), for example, and around university towns such as Missoula (Montana), Portland (Oregon), and Bellingham (Washington), many of the poets following in the tradition of the late Theodore Roethke at the University of Washington:

> the landing is always emotional
> in a tide running with us
> we all cry beautiful, Jesus, it's beautiful
> ("Nestucca River Poem," by Tom Crawford)

At the time the first *Geography* was put together, the liveliest opposition to the Northeast establishment was in the San Francisco Bay Area. For, beginning in the fifties and continuing through the seventies, San Francisco, with the explosion of Beat poetry, had become a challenge to the mandarins of the east—anti-academic, political, exuberant. In the forties and fifties, while Frank O'Hara and other poets of the New York School were surviving the gloomy McCarthyite days of the witch hunts and artistic shutdown by attaching themselves to the emerging Abstract-Expressionist art scene, Allen Ginsberg, Lawrence Ferlinghetti, Gregory Corso, and Jack Kerouac left the East for San Francisco's more benign climate. The birth of Beat poetry there caused a sensation around the country and the world, and affected poetry profoundly.

Today, beat poetry seems to have lost its leading role in the Bay Area, with some of the more interesting work coming from groups of ethnic-oriented poets at centers like the Kearny Street Workshop. And the torch of innovation has passed to the Long Beach/Los Angeles nexus, which sees America very differently from a Beat Scene focusing on "righteous" issues. In a landscape the rest of the country fantasizes about, Southern Californian poets largely ignore the unreal lure of the Hollywood mirage, orange groves, the surfer beaches, and Disneyland, and find their material more often in the somewhat sleazy realities of life, commemorating the survival of humanity among the sleaze, much as the poets of the New York School reflect in their poetry the garbagey life of the tenements around the fringes of the glossy corporate city.

In contrast to the near-operatic poetry of the Beats, with its language of incantation, hyperbole, even preaching, the new poetry from the L.A./Long Beach area is laid back, more related to talk than song, invoking stand-up comics, sassy comebacks, bartalk, and true confessions. As in the poetry of Charles Bukowski, the leading poet of the area, and notably the first American poet ever to write a major Hollywood movie (*Barfly*, starring Mickey Rourke and Faye Dunaway), cynicism is pervasive—love is often portrayed as alleycats fighting, and financial problems are never far away.

The bar, the racetrack, and porno shop are common settings, as are ethnic neighborhoods, or the banal atmosphere of a supermarket. The feminism that the women poets seem to be expressing is the independence to take and talk sex as forthrightly as men:

> Monday night. I'm at
> Safeway. I feel
> the honey dew and a man comes up, winks
> ("Hungry," by Lisa Glatt)

Poetry magazines, with names like *Pearl, Nausea, Marilyn, Little Caesar,* and *Poetry/LA* come and go, except for the best of them, Marvin Malone's long-surviving *The Wormwood Review.*

We have detached from Southern California the less populated, if geographically larger, Old West, because of its distinctive landscape of deserts and mountains, mining towns and cattle ranges, and its dominating Latino and Indian cultures:

> We heard the stories big-screen like,
> Martí did this, Sandino over there,
> Jara later without his fingers
> ("Singing the Internationale," by Alberto Rios)

Kirk Robertson, driving on an Indian reservation in Nevada, tells how:

> dust swirls behind you
> down Indian Lakes Road
> ("drawing to an inside straight")

As in all of America, this region contains ethnic diversity. With the same American voice that Texas-poet Naomi Shihab Nye uses to describe a cowboy at a bar while "the prairie rolls under the door," she must also express the suffering of her father's Palestinian countrymen:

> . . . this tragedy with a terrible root
> is too big for us. What flag can we wave?
> ("Blood")

One of the most important poetry centers in the Old West region is the Ruth Stephan Poets House at the University of Arizona in Tucson, which has a long tradition of visiting poets. Literary journals include the academically oriented *Western Humanities Review* in Salt Lake City, as well as numerous little magazines like *Yellow Brick Road* and *Scree*, and small publishers of poetry, such as Vergin' Press in West Texas and Duck Down Press in Nevada, among them.

In the Midwest, the vast center of the country, is located the dean of all writing workshops in the country and the model for almost all the writing programs adopted since— the Iowa Writers Workshop in Iowa City, around which several independent publishing houses have sprung up, such as Toothpaste Press, and The Spirit That Moves Us Press. Minneapolis/St. Paul is also an active center of poetry activity, with Coffee House and Greywolf notable among its small presses.

Poetry, the oldest poetry magazine in the country, founded in 1912, is still published in Chicago. Academic literary publications of the region, such as *Kansas Quarterly, Michigan Quarterly,* and *Iowa Review,* are balanced by a variety of independent journals that feature poetry: *Chiron Review, Dacotah Territory, Longhouse, Plainswoman, New American Writing, Pig Iron* in Youngstown, *Art Crimes* in Cleveland, among them. The University of Cincinnati, with its Elliston Poetry Room, and Cleveland State University's Poetry Center are only two of the many universities inviting known and less-known poets to their campuses.

Midwest poets portray life on the prairie as well as in the cities and factory towns. Shopping in Kansas, Jo McDougall finds herself feeling " . . . safe and not far/from the exact center of the United States." While Kathleen Norris of South Dakota writes of the women in her farm country:

> They laugh in the afternoon
> in a house set down
> on a God-forsaken, near-treeless plain.
>
> ("Pommes de Terre")

The same landscape evokes for Duane Niatum the tortured spirits of his ancestors:

> When Cheyennes, Iowas, and a Caddo step
> through the door in double leg-irons,
> without a trial or a hearing . . .
>
> ("Warrior Artists of the Southern Plains")

Social concerns are a major theme of rustbelt poets. Jim Daniels reports on the decay of his hometown:

> another abandoned house
> torched in Detroit,
>
> ("Watching My Old House Burn on the News")

A steel mill is seen by a child as a version of Hell:

> And the three warning whistle blasts,
> the blazing orange heat pouring out
> liquid fire like Devil's soup
>
> ("Field Trip to the Rolling Mill, 1950," by Patricia Dobler)

while Frank Polite of Youngstown, a graduate of the Iowa Writers' Workshop, laments:

> The fresh water goddess, Lake Erie,
> is dead.
>
> ("In My Black Book")

Illustrating the mobility of poets, transplanted Californian-poet Diane Wakoski can at last identify herself, as a

> . . . middle-aged
> mid-Western
> schoolteacher.
>
> ("The Ring of Irony")

The South, long the province of traditionalists, with its venerable trio of journals, *The Southern Review, Virginia Quarterly,* and the *Sewanee Review,* today has some of the livelier literary magazines in the country—among them, *Exquisite Corpse,* founded by Romanian emigré Andrei Codrescu in Baton Rouge (Louisiana), *Negative Capability* (Alabama), and at the University of Virginia the African-American quarterly, *Callaloo,* with its publishing imprint of the same name. Louisiana State University Press and University of Arkansas Press are also important publishers of new poetry, joined by smaller non-affiliated publishers like Beans and Brown Rice in Atlanta. New Orleans has poetry-reading series in many cafes and bookshops, with names like Ruby's Road House and Copastetic Book Center. And the University of Houston's Writing Center has a roster of leading poets.

In many southern writers we often sense the tradition that shapes their regional sensibility, as when Charles Wright writes of his "kinfolk" and the soil that nurtured him:

> . . . Aunt Roberta is still in town,
> Close to the place my great-great-grandfather taught
>   Nelly Custis's children once . . .
> Who cares? Well I do . . .
> It's worth my while to be here, crumbling this dirt
>   through my bare hands.
>
> ("Virginia Reel")

If these poets continue to remind us of their still-vivid Civil War memories, others point to the darker history of racial injustice, much of which, like in all parts of the country, remains:

Lo & behold. Yes, peat bogs
in Louisiana. The dead
stumble home like swamp fog,
our lost uncles & granddaddies

("Landscape for the Disappeared," by Yusef Komunyakaa)

And Miller Williams gives us another chapter of forgotten history from his boyhood in Arkansas during World War II:

When open trucks with German prisoners in them
passed in convoy through the small town
I dreamed in. . . .

("Wiedersehen")

From Florida, Peter Meinke writes of new immigrants to the region:

he can't read English. But he's one hell
of a fisherman—no one else
catches anything worth keeping while sleek
whiting agitate his pail. He can feed
an extended family tonight . . .

("The Vietnamese Fisherman on Tampa Bay")

The peculiar isolation of New York City and much of the Northeast literary establishment from the rest of the country is illustrated by a famous *New Yorker* cartoon in which the towers of Manhattan loom large in the foreground, while across the Hudson River the rest of the country quickly dwindles away in the distance. As in the cartoon, the cultural establishment continues to hold the view that there is nothing much going on "out there" that is worth paying attention to—though it is sometimes forced to do so. And it is true that this region still has the greatest concentration of poets in the country and the major publishing houses. But one of the most extensive publishing programs in the Northeast is carried on by the University of Pittsburgh Press, as well as by small poetry publishers like Sheep Meadow Press and Alice James Books.

One cannot entirely separate New York City from the rest of the Northeast, so, although we have made them two separate sections, it was unavoidable that the geographical concerns of our New York City poets would spill over the borders of the city into the country playgrounds that New Yorkers escape to, as in this observation of farmers by a New York poet:

> Workers outside my window in Long Island
> cut potatoes in pieces, bury them, water them.
>> ("Potato Song," by Stanley Moss)

But naturally the drama of the metropolis dominates. Here, James Schuyler reports:

> Coming from the deli
> a block away today I
> saw the UN building
>> ("This Dark Apartment")

which wasn't visible from his apartment windows.

And the subways exert as large a fascination to the poetic mind as any other feature of the New York landscape, as evidenced by the subway poems of Molly Peacock, Jack Anderson, and Sharon Olds, included here.

But the Northeast shares environmental concerns with the rest of the country:

> chemicals rising
> to the surface
> poison oozing up . . . ,
>> ("Love Canal," by Lyn Lifshin)

and has vivid memories of worker-parents:

> how at the end of his shift
> he'd come up from the pit in the gunboat,
> face black, lips and tongue pink . . .
>> ("My Mother at Evening," by Harry Humes)

Hometowns, as in the rest of the country, loom large. Here, Manuel Igrejas describes, with mixed feelings, the Ironbound section of Newark, where he grew up in the Portuguese colony as:

> a scrubbed ghetto of color and comfort
> where figs grow fat in tiny gardens
>
> ("Herois do Mar")

Whatever power games are played in the halls of the cultural establishment, the poets, in their poetry, are true to the observable life around them.

Here, then, is our *New Geography of Poets*, presenting a sampling of poets from every part of the United States, the most human and original of the poets we could find, perhaps still living in the places where they were born, or where they have ended up, or have found work for a while, and writing about it in their poetry—the native-born mixed with newcomers and transients, influencing each other, creating the mix, sometimes irreconcilable, even combustible, that is at the core of this country: The voices of the places.

What's That Smell in the Kitchen?

All over America women are burning dinners.
It's lambchops in Peoria; it's haddock
in Providence; it's steak in Chicago;
tofu delight in Big Sur; red
rice and beans in Dallas.
All over America women are burning
food they're supposed to bring with calico
smile on platters glittering like wax.
Anger sputters in her brainpan, confined
but spewing out missiles of hot fat.
Carbonized despair presses like a clinker
from a barbecue against the back of her eyes.
If she wants to grill anything, it's
her husband spitted over a slow fire.
If she wants to serve him anything
it's a dead rat with a bomb in its belly
ticking like the heart of an insomniac.
Her life is cooked and digested,
nothing but leftovers in Tupperware.
Look, she says, once I was roast duck
on your platter with parsley but now I am Spam.
Burning dinner is not incompetence but war.

Marge Piercy

THE
NORTHWEST

KIM ADDONIZIO

The Philosopher's Club

After class Thursday nights, the students
meet at the Philosopher's Club. It's right
around the corner from the streetcar tracks
at the West Portal tunnel. No one bothers
to check IDs. Five or six of them
get shooters and talk—about sex,
usually. Let me tell you about this dildo
I bought, one girl says. She describes
how it looks when all the gadgets
attached to it are going at once. My girlfriend
is pregnant, says one of the boys. That's
nothing, says another, I've got twins
I've never seen. It goes on like this
the whole semester. Gradually they learn
each other's stories: the girl raped
at knifepoint in Florida, the kid
whose old man shot seven people
in a trailer park outside Detroit.
Life is weird, they agree, touching glasses.
The bartender flips channels
on the TV, the sound turned down.
Spoiled brats, he thinks. He imagines a woman
with the blonde's legs, the brunette's tits.
"Dynasty" looks boring and he quits
at a black-and-white newsreel
about the Nazi camps—piles of heads
with their mouths open, bodies with arms
like chicken wings. On the jukebox
Otis Redding sings "Try a Little Tenderness."
One of the regulars stands there

3   THE NORTHWEST

popping his gum, jamming in selections.
The students, smashed, are hugging each other.
I love you, they all say. Outside, in the rain,
people are boarding a lit streetcar. As it jolts
towards the tunnel, some of them look back
at the bar, its staticky neon sign
the last thing they see as they enter the dark.

JAMES BROUGHTON

Aglow in Nowhere

At a meadow in Golden Gate Park
I stepped through an invisible gate
into the mellow light of nowhere
stepped beyond time and greenery

What had become of the seventy years
since first I tumbled on this grass?
And how many prices had I paid for
the tough somersaults that followed?

No longer brash nor intimidated
no longer riddled with wishes
I loll on this lawn of nowhere
and hope for a beatific vision

I know I have conquered nothing
I have simply outgrown everything
My history is a balloon I've let go of
without realizing I held on to it

Now I lack only a chamber for
what's left of my toys and scribbles
There I could desiccate quietly
like an Egyptian mummy   waiting
    for the last boat

TOM CRAWFORD

Nestucca River Poem

> *for Sarah, Quinton, and Marty*

When you come this far toward the mouth
the landing is always emotional
in a tide running with us
we all cry beautiful, Jesus, it's beautiful
and a blue sea answers back in waves
that are always arriving

I'm the first one ashore and in the ancient manner
claim this white spit for all of us
and all surrounding seas for miles
including the broken boat we later find
under a cliff
where cormorants hang their black wings out to dry

It is not an ordinary day
our feelings recorded in the smiles we can't hold back
in the ambivalent gestures our hands make
or in this poem
that doesn't begin to touch the salt grass
along this warm beach
or Sarah, bone tired, who cries to see a lone pelican
come into view

If there is sadness out here we brought it with us
in our summer clothes
and in the dim need we have
to make some claim on the truth

Me, I can't help it
I expect the drifting seal to talk,
the spit to rearrange itself with every tide
into another beautiful woman
Next time I'll be the broken boat
Hell, I know we are all dying
to come back
carrying some big human love
and skim like birds again over this sea water

WALT CURTIS

Skinnydipping on the Molalla River

for Tom and Marian

A naked silhouette,
he dove off the rock,
a very high rock,
into the green jewel
shadows of the river.

And came up spluttering
and splashing like a young whale.
Laughing with pleasure
and kicking his strong legs
as hard as he could
for the fun of it.

I had warned him about hidden rocks.
He looked and then dove
with typical determination.
What an indestructible youth!

There were natural pools here,
we were surrounded by green clean fir trees.
A pool of water—
What an exquisite word pool is!
The lips puff with pleasure before the plunge
into the green cold exhilarating water.

He came to the bank
where I was sitting naked.
I reached out my hand
and he pulled me in.
        Kersplash!
We bubbled up, caught our breath,
and swam to the sunlight
on the other side, upstream.

Sitting close in the sunlight,
water drops rolling down
        our bodies, he says
let's jump in the rapids
and swim downstream.

In we plunge.
I feel the undertow,
following the white frog
of his body, but make it
to the point of our return.
Scrambling out of the water,
and onto the rocks, catching our breath.

He is ready to go.
To another river.

Already putting on his boots,
naked above the ankles.
I say let me hold you,
and encircle my arms
and wet body around his.

Give me a kiss!
It's my birthday.
Laughingly
he french kisses me.
And hugs me
violently.
Feeling my hard-on
pressed against his
muscular body.

We take one last look
around, at the green river
and the forested canyon,
and then scramble
up the rugged bank.

The pregnant woman,
who was with us
and didn't want to go in the water,
has already gone on ahead.
He gives me one more
quick kiss, and I chase him
playing tag over the rocks
logs on the slippery slope
through the trees.

He beats me to the car.

SHARON DOUBIAGO

Signal Hill

My father leaves us in the car
and drinks beer in the Hilltop Bar.
The red neon woman who wears only
a ruffled apron and high heels
carries a tray of drinks
around and around the top of the hill
to the giant robots that pump
the fields.

In her red light my baby
brother and sister in the backseat of the car
are contorted in screams Daddy doesn't hear
over the jukebox and high squeals
of the bar maid I never see and wonder
if she too wears no clothes.
I hear her cry *ah Babes!*
We come here every Friday when he gets paid
but my brother and sister are still afraid
of the creatures nodding in the dark
we are parked between.

The city spreads beneath us
in a rainbow-spilled oil puddle.
The harbor is lit with battleships
that strain at their ropes
toward bigger war across the sea.

The dirty men keep driving up beside us.
I sit in the mother's seat
and they say to me things men say
to mothers.
I study her gay nipples

and wonder if mine will get that way.
Far below, on the shore of the Pike
a man sits on top of the neon needle
for months just to break a record.
One man says of him as he runs
his middle finger across the dewy window
of my face,
Tough, not gettin any.

When Daddy comes home through the door
beneath the spinning neon lady
it is the only time I ever see him
happy. Now we drive the cold side
of Signal Hill, the backside of the city and sea
so dark even now in the middle of the twentieth century
they hide the dying, the ones
they still can't cure, my mother
in her sanitarium.

We drive across the starry oil field
to her window where she lies
in the contagion ward we kids cannot go near.
My father taps on her dark window
and soon my mother lifts the pane
and puts her porcelain hand
out into the dark for him.

He puts one of his
on one of her large breasts
that are not like the red neon woman's
and sometimes lays his head
on her white arm that knows no sun
and between the groans of the field
letting go its oil
I hear him sigh
oh, honey, and sometimes
jesus

BARBARA DRAKE

When the Airplane Stopped

When Father's airplane stopped
and we were mid-air,
the little yellow Cub continued riding
along on chilly emptiness
like a boat in a stream.
Not a heavy thing at all,
it seemed a toy plane
of paper and balsa
tossed up with no rider
but the painted outline
of a soldier, his helmet
and goggles classic, his head
bent to the controls.

Father coughed and grinned
to a grimace, and I said, "Anything wrong?"
"Damn thing went off," he answered.

The bay looked long and blue and beautiful
against the sand spit;
the air was also blue, and chilly.
"Ice," said Father,
"in the carburetor."
And still we floated
in that nothingness,
with nothing to fear,
the nothing under us.

And Father fiddled with the starter
as the ailerons rowed space
and then before we'd really lost

much altitude, maybe none, maybe
we even gained some,
the engine started and Father smiled
and said, "I could land
this plane anywhere, engine or not:
a jetty, a dune, a country
highway. I could have taken it down."

The little plane coasted
along on its rutrutrut of an engine
till we landed where Mother sat
in the car at the railing,
and, "What were you doing up there?"
she asked us. "It looked funny."
We said,
"Flying."

Mother Said

Mother said, "Don't do it.
Once you do it
you have to go on doing it."
What kind of curse is that,
I wondered.
Hair will always grow back.
You will not have to go on the street
to keep yourself in razor blades.
Surely there is nothing final
about the loss of armpit hair virginity.

So I waited till one day
when mother was gone,

then made a hasty retreat to the tub.
Awash in gardenia bubble bath
and pine scented bath oil,
I lathered,
shaved,
dried and powdered
my armpits and legs,
wiped the prickly evidence off the porcelain,
put on a flowered nightie
and took my smooth little self to bed
with a book-of-the-month-club selection to read.

When mother came home,
came in to say good night,
I remarked (casually),
"Look what I did,"
and threw back the covers to show her,
fait accompli, my sleek legs.
I hadn't noticed the many cuts
which by now had bled and dried to the sheets.
It looked like a suicide attempt,
death by superficial laceration of the shins.

Mother looked peculiar and left the room.
Oh God, I thought,
now I have to
keep doing it.

LAWRENCE FERLINGHETTI

from *The Old Italians Dying*

For years the old Italians have been dying
all over America
For years the old Italians in faded felt hats
have been sunning themselves and dying
You have seen them on the benches
in the park in Washington Square
the old Italians in their black high button shoes
the old men in their old felt fedoras
                         with stained hatbands
have been dying and dying
                         day by day
You have seen them
every day in Washington Square San Francisco
the slow bell
tolls in the morning
in the Church of Peter & Paul
in the marzipan church on the plaza
toward ten in the morning the slow bell tolls
in the towers of Peter & Paul
and the old men who are still alive
sit sunning themselves in a row
on the wood benches in the park
and watch the processions in and out
funerals in the morning
weddings in the afternoon
slow bell in the morning Fast bell at noon
In one door out the other
the old men sit there in their hats
and watch the coming & going
You have seen them

the ones who feed the pigeons
                cutting the stale bread
                with their thumbs & penknives
the ones with old pocketwatches
the old ones with gnarled hands
                and wild eyebrows
the ones with the baggy pants
                with both belt & suspenders
the grappa drinkers with teeth like corn
the Piemontesi the Genovesi the Sicilianos
                smelling of garlic & pepperonis
the ones who loved Mussolini
the old fascists
the ones who loved Garibaldi
the old anarchists reading *L'Umanita Nuova*
the ones who loved Sacco & Vanzetti
They are almost all gone now
They are sitting and waiting their turn
and sunning themselves in front of the church
over the doors of which is inscribed
a phrase which would seem to be unfinished
from Dante's *Paradiso*
about the glory of the One
                who moves everything . . .
The old men are waiting
for it to be finished
for their glorious sentence on earth
                to be finished

TESS GALLAGHER

Legend with Sea Breeze

When you died I wanted at least to ring
some bells, but there were only clocks
in my town and one emblematic clapper
mounted in a pseudo-park for veterans.
If there had been bells I would have
rung them, the way they used to sound
school bells in the country so children
in my mother's time seemed lit
from the other side with desire
as they ran in from the fields
with school books over their shoulders.
Once more a yellow infusion of bells

empties like a vat of canaries into
the heart so it is over-full and
the air stumbles above roof tops, and death
in its naked quicksilver-echo shakes
our marrow with a yellow, trilling
silence. I would have given you that,
even though these nightshift mill workers,
these drinkers in childless taverns, these mothers
of daughters seduced at fourteen—what
can the language of bells say to them
that they haven't known first as swallows
blunting the breastbone. No, better

to lead my black horse into that grove
of hemlock and stand awhile. Better
to follow it up Blue Mountain Road
and spend the day with sword ferns,

with the secret agitations of creaturely
forest-loneliness. Or to forage
like a heat-stunned bear
raking the brambles for berries and thinking
only winter, winter, and of crawling
in daylight into the beautiful excess of earth
to meet an equal excess of sleep.
Oh my black horse, what's

the hurry? Stop awhile. I want to carve
his initials into this living tree.
I'm not quite empty enough to believe he's gone,
and that's why the smell of the sea
refreshes these silent boughs, and why
some breath of him is added if I mar the ritual,
if I put utter blackness to use
so a tremor reaches him as hoofbeats, as
my climbing up onto his velvet shoulders
with only love, thunderous sea-starved love,
so in the little town where they lived
they won't exaggerate when they say
in their stone-colored voices

that a horse and a woman flew down
from the mountain, and their eyes looked out
the same, like the petals of black pansies
school children press into the hollow
at the base of their throats as a sign
of their secret, wordless invincibility.
Whatever you do, don't let them ring any bells.
I'm tired of schooling, of legends, of
those ancient sacrificial bodies dragged to death
by chariots. I just want to ride my black horse,
to see where he goes.

Black Money

His lungs heaving all day in a sulphur mist,
then dusk, the lunch pail torn from him
before he reaches the house, his children
a cloud of swallows about him.
At the stove in the tumbled rooms, the wife,
her back the wall he fights most, and she
with no weapon but silence
and to keep him from the bed.

In their sleep the mill hums and turns
at the edge of water. Blue smoke
swells the night and they drift
from the graves they have made for each other,
float out from the open-mouthed sleep
of their children, past banks and businesses,
the used car lots, liquor store, the swings in the park.

The mill burns on, now a burst of cinders,
now whistles screaming down the bay, saws jagged
in half light. Then like a whip
the sun across the bed, windows high with mountains
and the sleepers fallen to pillows
as gulls fall, tilting
against their shadows on the log booms.
Again the trucks shudder the wood framed houses
passing to the mill. My father
snorts, splashes in the bathroom,
throws open our doors to cowboy music
on the radio, hearts are cheating,
somebody is alone, there's blood in Tulsa.
Out the back yard the night-shift men rattle
the gravel in the alley going home.
My father fits goggles to his head.

From his pocket he takes anything metal,
the pearl-handled jack knife, a ring of keys,
and for us, black money shoveled
from the sulphur pyramids heaped in the distance
like yellow gold. Coffee bottle tucked in his armpit
he swaggers past the chicken coop,
a pack of cards at his breast.
In a fan of light beyond him
the Kino Maru pulls out for Seattle,
some black star climbing
the deep globe of his eye.

ROBERT GLÜCK

The Chronicle

1

A swank luncheon thrown in Union Square by San
    Francisco
society's premiere hostess broke up today with apple cores
& curses & police drawing guns.

2

It was a catered affair featuring white gloved waiters,
staged by Charlotte Mailliard (pronounced Ma-yard) in
honor of I. Magnin exec. John Brunelle. A section of the
square was cordoned off & decorated with pastel balloons.

3

A bar was set up & drinks began pouring by noon. These
events excited considerable interest in onlookers, which

deepened as 40 guests sat down to spoon up their
vichyssoise, wash it down with chilled Pinot Blanc &
proceed to their avocados stuffed with shrimp.

4

90 minutes: murmurings turned to jeers: Rich Pigs Go
Home. Psychiatrist Richard Kunin, laying his napkin
down, rose to his feet & sought to reason.

5

"I told them, 'It can be painful being on the outside
looking in.' I said, 'I've been there before and I
suppose I will again.'" And by extension will they dine
one day at the table of Charlotte Mailliard? In this
way he bribed them with the distant mansions of country-
western music.

Personal Reflection

Dr. Kunin functions as the mediating idealogue. He
belongs to the echelon that works for its betters by
creating imaginary resolutions of real contradictions.
(For ex., Charlotte Mailliard remained blandly intact,
said "They were the entertainment.")

6

Jeers resumed & drowned out the music. The guests
uneasily swallowed their long-stemmed strawberries.
"We didn't want to lose face in front of the enemy."

7

When patrolmen Walsh & Scott arrived the first apple
cores were flying and the air was blue and red with curses
and rhetoric. They pulled their guns and shouldered their
way, politely saying "Excuse me, excuse me."

8

By this time the waiters were assembling the silver in
some haste. Charlotte Mailliard, who this week gave
a party for dogs, said Brunelle always wanted to eat lunch
there & never got the chance.

Personal Reflection

More interesting than her character is the question: what
forces generate interior landscapes of blackmail & cock-
tail
parties for dogs? When asked her view by the press the
rich rich rich Charlotte Mailliard answered: I give more
than I've received.

9

Three men were arrested. Two excaped. Nabbed: Richard
Sawyer, 26, unemployed truck driver from Susanville. He
called the *Chronicle* from City Prison: "I was just walking
through the park & saw all the people & the balloons &
the
police grabbed hold of me."

JIM GOVE

Meditating at Olema

up at the retreat in
the morning i would
go into a wooded
area sit on one of
three or four stumps

old tree sections cut
& placed as seats
for meditation &
the first morning a
rabbit

followed me up &
sat in the grass for
the hour i sat
quietly & the
rabbit was there

three mornings
watching me in my
meditation & once i
heard a whirring as if
the wind were

coming up & as i
rose up out of my
meditative state i
slowly opened my eyes
& squirrels

dozens of squirrels
were running around a
tree across the
clearing from where i
was sitting & a

day or so later i
was by myself & the
rabbit was gone &
the squirrels were
gone &

playing with my mind
i sed something like
if this is all as
real as it seems the
squirrels will be

back & i opened my
eyes & three
squirrels were
playing in the tree
& i went back

under for another ten
minutes or so &
then when i rose to
leave the animals
were gone the next

morning there were
deer

JANA HARRIS

We Fish Our Lives Out

On the boats all day
drinking.
Eight fishermen
and a galley table,
cups, half empty whiskey
tequila bottles,
cigarettes.

Talkin up big bucks
with the cannery women.
A couple of days ago
the skipper of the *Sea Spray*
fell overboard and drowned,
two years back
six men never got from the Elbow Room
to their bunks.
All look the same,
these beaches,
flat
the sea,
a desert
no one learns to swim in
and maybe just one body washes
ashore.
We don't just talk fishin,
we fish,
fish all the trips we've ever been on.
Fish the world, do decades of fishing
in a whiskey bottle
at the galley table.
We fish our lives out,
drink
crash
wake up
leave at 6, drink
fish till dark.

Norma at the A&W Drive-In

Me and Rhonda draggin the strip
goin to the A&W drive-in
to watch Rhonda's ex sister-in-law

Norma
rollerskate her big butt around
car to car.
We'd order a mamaburger
and bloody fingers "to go"
wipin the catsup and french fry grease
all over the tray
so Norma'd have to clean it up.
Sayin she was havin *another* kid
ruinin Rhonda's good family name.
Laughin, sayin she oughta call this one TARGET
cause every guy in Molalla'd
had a shot at it.
Talkin about Norma being four months pregnant
and Rhonda's Ma *even* asked her
if there was anythin she needed
to walk down the aisle.
But there goes Norma
with a giant run in her nylons—
and every one of Rhonda's family
was so embarrassed
they coulda died.

ROBERT HASS

Name as the Shadow of the Predator's Wing

They bulldozed the upper meadow at Squaw Valley
where mist rose from mountain grasses on summer
    mornings
and a few horses grazed through it in the early heat,
where moonrise threw the owl's shadow on the wood rat
and the vole crouched and not breathing in the sage smell

the earth gave back with the day's heat to the night air.
And when they had gouged up the deep-rooted bunch-
    grass
and the wet alkali-scented earth had been pushed aside
or trucked someplace out of the way, they poured con-
    crete
and laid road—pleasant smell of tar in the spring sun—
and when the framers had begun to pound nails,
and the electricians and plumbers came around to talk
    specs
with the general contractor, someone put up a green sign
with alpine daisies on it that said Squaw Valley Meadows.

Adhesive: For Earlene

How often we overslept
those gray enormous mornings
in the first year of marriage
and found that rain and wind
had scattered palm nuts,
palm leaves, and sweet rotting crabapples
across our wildered lawn.

By spring your belly was immense
and your coloring a high rosy almond.

We were so broke
we debated buying thumbtacks
at the Elmwood Dime Store
knowing cellophane tape would do.
Berkeley seemed more innocent
in those flush days
when we skipped lunch
to have the price of *Les Enfants du Paradis*.

SUSAN KENNEDY

Dancing with the Dog

in the deep dark of December
feeling fat and cynical, I reach
for the radio, out pulses sweet
rockin' reggae, warm Caribbean breeze . . .
Rufus rises from his rug in front of the fire,
noses my thigh with wet chocolate nose,
yellow-gold hound eyes pleading, "Come on,
let's dance!"
once in a kind of trance
out of the corner of my eye
I saw him enter the room
six feet tall with a red beard
a ruddy Renaissance courtier
sent back in this life as our hound—
yesterday I caught him watching Michael and me
making love on the couch, his eyes filled with such a
melancholy yearning I had to put him out . . .
o.k. Rufus, give me your gorgeous powerful paws,
let's dance!

CAROLYN KIZER

Promising Author

Driving on the road to Stinson Beach
I remember your witty gap-toothed face
Half-ruined in a dozen shore-leave brawls,
And the straw hair and softening gut
Of a beat-up scarecrow out of Oz.

I drove this road with you
Some sixteen years ago
Skidding on curves between the pepper trees.
You whipped the wheel as though it were a helm
And laughted at my nauseated pleas.

Once at the beach you made the finest soup
I've ever tasted: scallops, peas and leeks,
And I pictured you, the cook on some old tramp
Scudding through Conrad seas,
A boy still dazzled by his luck and grace.

Later that week, in Sausalito's
Bar with no name, I watched you curl your lip
As you ran down every writer in the place,
Unkinder with each drink,
Till I fled up the hill to the French Hotel.

After that you married Beth, so rich
She bought you monogrammed silk shirts,
A dozen at a clip,
You wore as you sneered at your shabby friends
Who had lent you money.

You became glib as any Grub Street hack,
Then demanded help
To write the novel you would never write:
As I turned you from the door
You cursed me, and I cursed you back.

Once I believed you were the great white shark,
Slick predator, with tough scarred hide.
But now I know you were a small sea-lion,
Vulnerable, whiskery, afraid,
Who wept for mercy as you died.

DORIANNE LAUX

Ghosts

It's midnight and a light rain falls.
I sit on the front stoop to smoke.
Across the street a lit window, filled
with a ladder on which a young man stands.
His head dips into the frame each time
he sinks his brush in the paint.

He's painting his kitchen white, patiently
covering the faded yellow with long strokes.
He leans into his work like a lover, risks
losing his balance, returns gracefully
to the precise middle of the step

to dip and start again.

A woman appears beneath his feet, borrows
paint, takes it onto her thin brush
like a tongue. Her sweater is the color
of tender lemons. This is the beginning
of their love, bare and simple
as that wet room.

My hip aches against the damp cement.
I take it inside, punch up a pillow
for it to nest in. I'm getting too old
to sit on the porch in the rain,
to stay up all night, watch morning
rise over rooftops.

        Too old to dance
circles in dirty bars, a man's hands

laced at the small of my spine, pink
slingbacks hung from limp fingers. Love.
I'm too old for that. The foreign tongues
loose in my mouth, teeth that rang
my breasts by the nipples like soft bells.

I want it back. The red earrings and blue
slips. Lips alive with spit. Muscles
twisting like boat ropes in a hard wind.
Bellies for pillows. Not this ache in my hip.

I want the girl who cut through blue poolrooms
of smoke and golden beers, stepping out alone
into a summer fog to stand beneath a street lamp's
amber halo, her blue palms cupped
around the flare of a match.

She could have had so many lives. Gone off
with a boy to Arizona, lived on a ranch
under waves of carved rock, her hands turned
the color of flat red sands. Could have said
yes to a woman with fingers tapered as candles,
or a man who slept in a canvas tepee, who pulled
her down on his mattress of grass where she made
herself as empty as the gutted fire.
                              Oklahoma.
I could be there now, spinning corn from dry
cobs, working fat tomatoes into mason jars.

The rain has stopped. For blocks the houses
drip like ticking clocks. I turn off lights
and feel my way to the bedroom, slip cold
toes between flowered sheets, nest my chest
into the back of a man who sleeps in fits,
his suits hung stiff in the closet, his racked
shoes tipped toward the ceiling.

This man loves me for my wit, my nerve,
for the way my long legs fall from hemmed skirts.
When he rolls his body against mine I know
he feels someone else. There's no blame.
I love him, even as I remember a man with cane-
brown hands, palms pink as blossoms opening
over my breasts.
                    He holds me,
even with all those other fingers wrestling
inside me, even with all those other shoulders
wedged above his own like wings.

COLLEEN J. MCELROY

With Bill Pickett at the 101 Ranch

he was wilder than a wolf when he brought
down a steer with his teeth

but working the 101 was a damn sight better
than riding herd through Kansas winters
snow higher than the haunches of his best horse, Spradley
and his face, if not burnt summer black, matching his
        saddle

"damn that colored feller can bull-dawg" they said
when the bull whip-snapped his body like a twig

the crowd of Shoshone stragglers and coon-tailed
mountain men cheered this brush cowpoke

who earned his keep by his teeth, but when he turned
show biz and rode the 101 with Tom Mix

camp bosses with red beards and grey eyes
grew nervous to see what he could do

what he could do was judge the angle of light
against ground swell of mud from gate to center post

despite old rope burns that hummed memories to his
    bones
he listened as calves moaned in the holding pens

and longhorns bellowed at the sound of his footsteps as if
they knew how his hands were rubbed raw against horns

how he bit the bull's lip until the beast caved in
and how his own blood smelled worse than puke and
    dung

worse than the scent of death in the air
the crowd cheering bull against man
and hoping, dear God, the beast would win

JANICE MIRIKITANI

Jade

The woman insisted
my name must be Jade.
Your name's not Jade?
Well, it should be.
It suits you, jewel of the orient.

I knew a young hooker
called Jade.
She had red dyed hair
and yellow teeth

bucked around a perpetual candy bar.
They called her Jade
because she was Clyde's
jewel of the orient.
Her real name was Sumiko . . .
Hardy or Johnson or Smith.
She was from Concord.
Boring, she said,
and kept running away
from home. Her father
would come looking for her,
beat her again,
drag her home
while her mother
babbled and bawled in Japanese.
Concord was boring.
Jade kept running away,
Clyde's jewel of the orient.
He took care of her well,
and she couldn't wait
to see him, her hunger
like locusts in drought,
to put the cold needle to her vein,
blood blossoming in the
dropper like bougainvillea
pushing the heroin through,
her eyes exploding with green lights,
the cold encasing
each corpuscle,
rushing through
heart to the spine,
a freeze settling in each
vertebra until
she's as cold as stone,
metabolism at zero degrees,
speech center numbed

and life as still as icicles.
Pain, boredom, loneliness
like a frosty pillow
where she lays her nodding
head.
                    I wanted to tell
                    the woman who kept
                    insisting my name was Jade
about Jade.
who od'd. Her jaundiced body
found on her cold floor
mattress,
roaches crawling in her ears,
her dead eyes, glassy
as jewels.

RALPH POMEROY

River's End

We had to stop.
Pulling the car over,
High above the ocean,
The late light compelled us.
Promise of sunset,
Perfect day.

Finally,
After a scary drive
Across the mountains
From St. Helena

Over endless dirt roads,
Menaced by huge logger trucks,
Light lowering,
Without sight of the sea
We both knew
Had to be there.

All the more reason for rejoicing
When we got to the highway
And a place called Fish Rock.
We drove until we reached
The scenic pull-off at Jenner
Where the Russian River flows
Into the Pacific.

Far below, I saw—and
Couldn't believe my eyes at first—
A colony of seals
Basking on a sandbar.
You didn't believe my eyes either
Until you saw the seals for yourself,
Lying in the last brilliant sunlight
Some teaching their pups to swim.

We vowed to return
When you had more time
And walk the long way down
To the spot where the seals taught.

That night we had a fish dinner
At a funky restaurant
Named "Nick's Cove"—
You, local oysters.

That was our coastal trip
North of San Francisco

Which I'd always wanted
You to experience.
A few days later
You mounted your Harley
And headed back East
To New York.

In Utah, you had
The accident.

◆ ◆ ◆

Now,
A year later,
I've returned.
The river,
The ocean,
The seals,
Are all here.

You too
Are absolutely here
With me,
Within me.

Together,
We begin the long walk down.

Our vow kept.

KAREN RANDLEV

The Sound of Drums

Having held me in their thrall for years now,
the sound of drums thrums in my ears.
Neither Denali nor the Chukchi,
not fireweed not the ptarmigan,
come to mind when I remember the North;
drum sounds echo in my head.
Old men come into sight as their kamiks
pat the floor; old Inupiat women
smooth the air as they danced
in the social hall many years ago.
Nowadays I hear jets and traffic noise,
factory buzz and garbage men,
clanging early morning.

Progress

I first went to Fairbanks in '76,
it was the height of the pipeline,
but it didn't hit me until this cute guy
offered me some Juicy Fruit in the Coop Drugstore
on Two Street. Those were the days.
I'd never seen a summer so long;
The sky came right down to the land;
it was hot as hell. For all that
I put my house on the Market, packed
up the dog and my kid, and drove up the Alcan
from Seattle to Tok.
I lasted six years.

When I went back to Fairbanks,
catching food poisoning from potato salad
on the way—throwing up in the john
of the Budget Rent-a-Car on Airport Road,
things weren't the same.
Those sweet Juicy Fruit guys were gone,
Two Street was trying for respectable,
and every corner had a shopping mall
selling pistachio nuts and gourmet-delites
from the lower '48.
I couldn't stay as long this time;
I turned in my cheap Super Saver
for a regular tourist fare and fled.
The fireweed was still there, but even the hippies
on Chena Pump looked like Berkeley.
It was time to go home.

CARLOS REYES

Moon Mullins

The first time I met him
we were headed out of Newport
for the Columbia bar.
He came up the doghouse
took out the chart
ruler and a number four pencil
drew a heavy line roughly North
and said this is the way we'll go boys
and disappeared below.

I believe he once said
when I was with him

that the surface of the sea
was rolling hills green and sometimes
blue where goats or maybe he said boats
gamboled and frolicked
sometimes in the bright sunshine
sometimes hiding behind waves in the fog.

And I think I once heard him call
the seaweed that collected on the lines
goatsbeard or maybe he was just mumbling
or maybe it was a bit untranslated
from his native language
whatever that was. Well

the thing I'm certain he said
the one thing he was right about
was that the ocean has a face
angry or smiling and you can read it
but you'd better read it right.

VERN RUTSALA

Northwest Passage

Out past Sylvan Beach is the place
They still call Indian Village
Built only to be burned
The summer Spencer Tracy came to town

For years after that
Whole families would picnic there
Scavenging debris
For rubber arrowheads

But when Spencer came
Everyone got jobs
Five dollars a day and lunch
The Depression ending with glamour

And the chance to sew on a button
For a star
Some of the men were extras
Growing beards and wearing buckskin

Rogers' Rangers looking for that passage
All summer long
From eight to five
My father was among them

And once years later
The summer after he died
I saw the movie on the late show
I stared at it hard

Even recognized a few landmarks
I scavenged every frame
For the smallest sign of him
I found none

WILLIAM STAFFORD

Roll Call

Red Wolf came, and Passenger Pigeon,
the Dodo bird, all the gone and endangered
came and crowded around in a circle,
the Bison, the Irish Elk, waited
silent, the Great White Bear, fluid and strong,

sliding from the sea, streaming and creeping
in the gathering darkness, nose down,
bowing to earth, its tapered head,
where the Black-footed Ferret, paws folded,
stood in the center surveying the multitude
and spoke for us all: "Dearly beloved," it said.

WILLIAM TALCOTT

Boogie Board

for August Kleinzahler

I'm looking for the three
hundred block so I can drop

off some poems. I get off
the 71 & walk over to Cole.
I lived here that famous
summer, children asleep

in stairwells. I'd step
over them on the way to State

College. The kid next door
heard bubbles & tripped out,

knocked on our door. She
cradled him as if she were about

to nurse him but she didn't. Hey,
there's the tiger house

looking fierce & green today.
The address a few doors up.

Bye-bye poems & I head for
Belvedere. Uncomfortable name.

Apollo or that place
near Tiburon. But the sun's

warm for January.
I talk with a woman carrying

a boogie board then walk down
to Haight & the Booksmith where I

buy *A Calendar of Airs* & I say
he lives around here doesn't he

to the clerk who says yes
he was in this morning.

JOANNE TOWNSEND

Something That Has to Do With . . .

After two weeks in Western Alaska,
my house seems strange at first and too quiet.
Winds don't chomp at its outer angles,
the water pump is indecently silent.

Travel weary, I toss, sleep fitfully,
dream once more of the Yupik woman in the birdskin
    parka.
This time I think I see her
outline against the tundra's blowing snow.

Come in, come in, I shout. Rest awhile.
It's warm inside. There's hot tea.
But the lost one drifts into white glare.
I wake.

From the near gray wall begging paint,
my crippled aunt, dead these twelve years,
looks down at me from a tortoise shell frame.
She's wearing her formal crepe with the beaded fuschia
    yoke,
the dress I remember, and this too—

> August 1969, I went East with my baby.
> Dog days, 94 degrees, and the washer gave out.
> Auntie wouldn't let me go to the laundromat;
> she got out the washboard and Fels Naptha,
> filled the tub,
> rested her pronged cane against the porcelain sink,
> scrubbed every diaper by hand.

Suddenly I want those speckled hands to rest in mine,
want those paper lips to move.
There's something I need to ask her,
something that has to do with grown babies and trouble,
something that has to do with limping and canes.

Up the street
seagulls jostle over fish scraps from the cannery,
my neighbor revs his Winnebago, a jet buzzes the roof.
Anchorage morning. Stiffly I step into the front room.
The dog jumps a welcome and when the phone rings,
I answer guardedly, Hello, hello, hello . . .
There is only static.

DAVID WAGONER

My Father's Football Game

He watched each TV game for all he was worth, while
    swaying
Off guard or around end, his jaw
Off center. He made each tackle
Personally, took it personally if the runner broke through
To a broken field. He wanted that hotshot
Down, up and around and down
Hard, on the ground, now, no matter which team was
    which.

Star backs got all the cheers. Their names came rumbling,
    roaring
Out of grandstands from the loud mouths
Of their fathers. He'd show them
How it felt out cold for a loss, to be speared, the pigskin
Fumbled and turned over. Man
To man he would smile then
For the linemen, *his* team, the scoreless iron men getting
    even.

But if those flashy legs went flickering out of the clutches
Of the last tackler into the open
Past anyone's goal line, he would stand
For a moment of silence, bent, then take his bitter cup
To the kitchen, knowing time
Had been called for something sweeter
Than any victory: he would settle down to his dream game

Against Jim Thorpe and the Carlisle Indians for
    Washington
& Jefferson, buddy, that Great Year

By George Nineteen Sixteen
In mud, sweat, and sleet, in padding thinner than chain
   mail,
With immortal guts and helmets
Flying, the Savages versus the Heroes
By failing light in a *Götterdämmerung,* Nothing to Nothing.

AL YOUNG

California Peninsula: El Camino Real

In 15 minutes
the whole scenell change
as bloated housewives
hems of their skirts greased
with love mouths wide open
come running out of shops
dragging their young
moon in their eyes
the fear upon them

Any minute now
the gas-blue sky over El Camino Real
is going to droop for good
shut with a squish &
close them all in like
a giant irritated eye

Theyll scramble for cars
the nearest road out
clutching their steering wheels
like stalwart monkeys

It couldve happened yesterday
It couldve happened while they
were sighing in Macy's Walgreen's 31 Flavors
Copenhagen Movies or visiting the Colonel
like that earthquake night
that shattered L.A.

Whatll they will their children then?
Whatll they leave for them to detest?
What tree, what lip print, what Jack in
what Box, what ugly hot order to go?

Already I can smell the darkness
creeping in like the familiar shadow
of some beloved fake monster
in a science fiction flick

In 15 minutes
48 hours days weeks months
years from now all of thisll be
a drowsy memory barely tellable
in a land whose novelty was speech

THE
MIDWEST

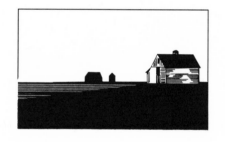

ANTLER

The Discovery of Lake Michigan

Canoeing down a graceful willow-lined river
      to its mouth,
Or hiking through forest parting high brush
      on some steep bluff,
Or struggling over sand dunes
      smelling water,
Suddenly the original happener-on-er
      gazing at the endless blue!

One night at twilight the first human being
      to stand on the shore of Lake Michigan
Stood on the shore of Lake Michigan
      and took a drink from a wave.
She'd never seen a body of water so big.
Perhaps this was the end of the Earth,
Perhaps this Ocean stretched on
      forever.

How many centuries passed
Before someone courageous enough
      tried canoeing across it and returned?
Whoever it was must have been regarded as
      the Columbus of Lake Michigan,
But those people didn't call it Lake Michigan
And before humans came
      Lake Michigan had no name.

JIM BARNES

from *An Ex-Deputy Sheriff Remembers
the Eastern Oklahoma Murderers*

i. Summerfield

They took a tire tool to his head,
this gentle stranger from Wyoming.
Oh, we caught them over
at Talihina drinking beer
at Lester's Place, calling
the myna bird bad names
and shooting shuffleboard.
I'm telling you
they were meek in the muzzle
of our guns. They claimed innocence
and: why, they went fishing
with the Cowboy just the other day.
We said we knew, knew too
the way they stole him blind
that night. We spoke of blood,
the way the dogs had lapped his face.
The youngest of the three bad brothers,
barely thirteen, began to cry:
"He told us everything was all right
and we hit him till he died."
And that is how it was,
a simple thing, like breathing,
they hit him until he died,
until he bled Wyoming dry
there on the road
in that part of Oklahoma
no stranger has ever owned.

ii. Red Oak

We shot the Choctaw way back in '94,
last legal execution by firing squad.
He didn't die, through the heart, square
and he didn't die.
The high sheriff, my old boss,
stuffed his own shirt down
the Choctaw's neck
to stop the rattle in his throat.
You couldn't shoot a downed man
no matter what and he had to die.
Damned good Choctaw, I'll say that.
Red Oak had no jail and it was too
blasted cruel to execute him
before his crop was in. The judge
scheduled it for the fall, first Saturday
after the corn was in the Choctaw's crib.
That damned fool Choctaw gathered
his corn like any other dirt farmer,
dressed clean, and kept his word.
"I'm ready" is all he said that day.
You got to admire a man like that,
Indian or not, murderer or just plain fool.
He'd shot three men for sleeping
in his barn and taking the milk bucket
away from his little girl, though she
wasn't harmed at all, and he showed up
just like he'd said he would.

                    There
was a picnic in the shade after we choked
the Choctaw to death and took the rifle home.
First time I'd ever seen a camera,
big damned black thing on legs,
smelled like seven kinds of sin every time
it popped. Had fresh hominy and chicken and the last
of some damned fine late sweet red watermelons.

DAVID CITINO

Visiting My Father in Florida

Forty years, every working day he drove
through the roiling haze of Cleveland streets
to the Harshaw Chemical Co., past Union Carbide,
Rockwell International, Bethlehem Steel, all the
barbed-wire, bricked-windowed plants, sulfur
rising from their stacks to rain on playgrounds
and reservoirs, the states downwind. He knew

the neighborhoods of Italians and Poles, Greeks
and Slovenes, Slovaks and Croats before they moved
their kitchen tables, photo albums and ceramic jockeys
to the suburbs. He couldn't understand the girls
in platform heels and slit skirts who'd whisper
"Hey Mister" from bleak doorways. "Go home to
your mother," he told one once. "Your white ass,"

she answered. He persisted so long even he changed.
Now we drive through his new "planned community,"
banks and K Marts garish as modern churches,
acres of offices of oncologists, proctologists,
urologists, ancient women pedaling tricycles,
Lincoln and Cadillac dealers, the old in bunches
raising blouses and shirts to show their latest scars.

Later we fish this new canal. Caloosahatchee mullet
leap stiffly toward the sky. He lifts his rod
and a whiskered, flat-headed catfish the color
of sludge lands between us, writhing. I've never
seen a thing so old, so ugly, It leaves a trail
of slime on the new dock, lost in so much sudden light,
blind. Its mouth gulps the precious, useless air.

Volare

Just as lights inside our living room
and steam from water boiling on the stove
erase Cleveland from the picture window,
father comes in,
stands in the kitchen, one shoulder thrust forward,
feet apart the way he's seen Lanza stand,
eyelids drooping like Dean Martin's or Como's,
Lucky Strike stuck to lower lip.
We can leave the confusion
and all disillusion behind.
And we know he got the raise,
his laborer's share of chemical company profits
from the Manhattan Project
and the revolution in plastics.
Four hundred a year. And that's not hay.
He grabs my mother
and spins with her before the stove,
wooden spoon brandished like the fine lady's fan
she saw that day in pages of *Life.*
Just like birds of a feather
a rainbow together we'll find.
Then he comes for me,
and I'm soaring above cauldrons
of rigatoni and sauce bubbling bright
as the scarlet cassocks altar boys wear
at Christmas and Easter.
He brings me back to earth
and twirls away to phone his mother.
That night when he comes home from moonlighting
in the credit department at Sears,
feet heavy as bricks,
he'll come to my bedroom and tell me again
how there'll be no promotion for him
because he couldn't go to college

but still he's risen higher than his father
who put in fifty years with the B&O.
He'll step out the door
and for a moment his head will be caught in light
like some raptured hoary saint drunk on love
in the window of Ascension of Our Lord
and the last thing I'll hear
will be his lovely forlorn baritone
fading, fading into stillness.
Volare. Wo-wo. Cantare. Wo-o-o-o.

PHILIP DACEY

The Feet Man

The worst job I ever had was nailing
Jesus' feet to the cross on the
assembly line at the crucifix factory.
Jesus! I'd never thought of myself
as religious before that, but when
I had to strike those nails—I figured
it up once—more than two thousand times
a day, my mind began seeing things:
little tremors along the skin, jerks of
those legs that were bonier than
models' legs, his eyes imploring,
forgiving. I swear, if a tiny drop of blood
had oozed out of that wood at my pounding,
I wouldn't have been surprised at all.
I was ripe for a miracle, or a vacation.
All I got was worse: with each blow
of the hammer, I flinched, as if I

were the one getting pierced. Doing
that job day after day was bad enough,
but doing it to myself—my arms
spread out from one end of my paycheck
to the other—was crazy. I began
to sweat constantly, though the place
was air-conditioned. It wasn't long before
the foreman took me aside and told me
I was taking my job too seriously, that
if I wanted to keep it I had better calm down.
He was right. I pulled myself together
like a man and put all pointless thoughts
out of my head. Or tried to. It wasn't easy:
imagine Jesus after Jesus coming down
at you along that line, and you with
your hammer poised, you knowing
what you have to do to make a living.

JIM DANIELS

Watching My Old House Burn on the News

A sixty-second spot:
another abandoned house
torched in Detroit,
a slow day for news.

Water shoots from the hoses,
mixes with a light rain.
A bunch of kids stand nearby
mugging for the camera.

No bodies to carry out, nothing
to save. The firemen
keep it from spreading.
My mother cries.

On the sheets of a tired bed
in the upper flat of that house
I was conceived
on a wet night like this,

September, rain knocking
leaves from the trees,
two babies crying
in the other room.

My mother's tears fall tonight
not like that rain at all
not like those falling leaves.
Like those flames. Like that fire.

PATRICIA DOBLER

Field Trip to the Rolling Mill, 1950

Sister Monica has her hands full
timing the climb to the catwalk
so the fourth-graders are lined up
before the next heat is tapped, "and no
giggling no jostling, you monkeys!
So close to the edge!" She passes out
sourballs for bribes, not liking
the smile on the foreman's face,

the way he pulls at his cap,
he's not Catholic. Protestant madness,
these field trips, this hanging from catwalks
suspended over an open hearth.

Sister Monica understands Hell
to be like this. If overhead cranes clawing
their way through layers of dark air
grew leathery wings and flew screeching
at them, it wouldn't surprise her.
And the three warning whistle blasts,
the blazing orange heat pouring out
liquid fire like Devil's soup
doesn't surprise her—she understands
Industry and Capital and Labor,
the Protestant trinity. That is why
she trembles here, the children clinging
to her as she watches them learn their future.

GARY GILDNER

The Porch

Sometimes it happens
I am having a good time
just sitting on the porch
in my big brown rocker
watching the sky sneak by.

Maybe smelling the dirt
I had turned over and raked
clean for my beans

a while ago, my body feeling
used and grateful.

Or maybe recalling a long spidery
girl I had clambered up
the sand dunes with
in Michigan once, her shoulders softly
freckled by the sun.

And maybe beyond the geranium,
perched in the wild
black raspberry patch
its mother pushed it into,
there's a young speckled robin.

fat and crabby-
looking, looking
and rocking
a little,
same as me.

Sometimes it happens
the retired gentleman
across the alley will slip
into his old
green Mercury,

tip the snappy red lid
to the back of his head,
and listen to her
purr
for a spell.

And sometimes it happens
while I'm rocking here
feeling used and lucky

and happy in my juices,
that nothing happens—

the sycamores stand,
the shade does its usual
slow business
with the leaves
over my bare toes,

and easily,
oh how easily
I fall asleep
and dream of
almost touching you.

LAURENCE GOLDSTEIN

Ann Arbor Solitary

Brawling in the bush with himself
our schnapps-bloated German
punches free to the sidewalk,
mock-orange blossoms in both fists.
His bright yellow blazer, a sign
of bad conscience—for we know
his taste is good, and bottomless—
turns every human head.
It's twilight, his only happy hour.

New faculty have made Germantown
a ghetto of sorts, him a survivor.
He once let drop that my house

havened a devotee of the Führer
who carpentered for the old families.
I imagine these compatriots in song—
swelling the *Horst Wessel Lied,* and
chiming steins at The Heidelberg.

Having nothing on these blocks
to remember, I remember a ghost
who safeguarded the pine floors
and surely gazed with pleasure upon
the celtic patterns of the woodwork,
the chalet-style gingerbread,
the Nordic newel post and moldings
he mined with coverage of the Last Days
when he repaired what I re-repair.

Often I fancy a bull shape
snorting like my sodden neighbor's,
a distemper passionate as his,
eager to trespass and reclaim,
their voices mingled into one
that calls to my boys at catch
across the battlement of spirea,
"Here was a piece of the Fatherland."

JIM GUSTAFSON

The Idea of Detroit

Detroit just sits there
like the head of a large dog on a serving platter.
It lurks in the middle of a continent,
or passes itself off as a civilization
at the end of a rope.

The lumpiness of the skyline
is the lumpiness of a sheet stretched over
what's left of a tender young body.
Detroit groans and oppresses.
It amounts to Saturday night at the slaughter house,
and Sunday morning in bed
with a bag of bagels and the Special Obituary
    Supplement.
Air the color of brown Necco wafers,
a taste like the floor of an adult movie theater,
the movement through the streets
that of a legless, wingless, pigeon.
Detroit means lovers buying matching guns,
visitors taken on tours of the foundries,
children being born with all their teeth,
a deep scarlet kind of fear.
It breeds a unique bitterness,
one that leaves deep gashes in the tongue,
that doesn't answer telephones or letters,
that carves notches in everything,
that illustrates the difference between
"rise up singin" and "sit down and shut your face."
It forms a special fondness for uncooked bacon,
for the smell of parking lots,
for police sirens as opposed to ambulance sirens,
for honest people who move their heads
whenever they move their eyes.
Detroit is a greasy enchilada
smeared across the face of a dilemma,
the sanctuary of the living dead,
the home of the Anywhere-But-Here travel agency,
the outhouse at the end of the rainbow.
Detroit just sits there
drinking can after can of Dupe beer,
checking the locks on the windows,
sighing deeply, knowing that nothing
can save it now.

CHRISTOPHER HOWELL

Mean and Stupid

Ricky Stoppard died
in a slimey, undulent tangle
near the south face of a strip mine
outside Wier, Kansas.
That was where the snakes
caught up to him, praying
too loudly and taking the Lord's name
at the same time.
That was how it was.
All the Baptist farmers
hereabouts will tell you
it was a low-down
two-talking son of a loafing skunk
who died that day (riddance be praised!);
that Ricky stank corn liquor,
cursed life, had once attempted armed robbery
of a charity bazaar in Girard, and that the snakes
were instruments of a judgment
others had been making for a long time before the
    Almighty
at last threw the machineries of balance
into gear. Rumor
has it, too, that Ricky, when he fell
into the fateful waters of reptilian vengeance,
called out for someone to toss him
a brick; thereby adding stupidity to the list of charges.
I've seen his gravestone and it reads:

> RICKY STOPPARD
> 1953–1985
> Mean & Stupid

I'm standing by that tombstone
and my hat is off
to his terrible death
and a life of miserable small crimes
poorly made. I pray I may be spared
the pain and heat of Ricky's soul
that sighed like a rotten wagon wheel
and broke. And I pray for that
soul, the Old Nick of it somehow
near to me as love
or yearning
or any lost equation none of us will ever finally
get. I can hear the night freight
mourning through Riverton
as farmhouse lights die out below the darker
owls circling, flagrantly
disdainful of the Oklahoma line, and Ricky's cruel
headstone comes undone. He's finished now, at least,
and he's all right (being gone). The wind and blown
leaves clatter and agree; at least
he's not all wrong.

LORRI JACKSON

July in Chicago

downtown pigeons peck at dirty
bits on the roof of the ymca
on chicago & state
where i live
in so much uncertainty
now in the clinging heat

of a downhill july
after having jumped
the sinking cardboard boat
of love & frustration
from a man
only a man, twisted
w/ his fear & helplessness
it is easy to throw down
what you cannot possess; target
of flesh, my lips still
bare the scars of splits
direct hits
and so i land
in this place of tired history
where i meet old tumors
ready to pass on the buck
who talk of cafeterias
filled in the early mornings
w/ the relief of junkies
who have made it through again
of corner rooms, shooting
speed, of blackouts
that wake a man up
on the 20th floor, his fingers around
a black whore's throat
as she gags
as he tries to hit her
in the jugular, the only place left
not hard and inpenetrable

WILLIAM KLOEFKORN

I Had Been Chained and Padlocked

I had been chained and padlocked
and snapped to the clothesline
because I called my brother
a son of a bitch.
*Then let's see how much you enjoy
being one of my puppies,*
mother said,
and by evening,
when father came home from work,
I was barking almost deliciously
through the savage salt in my tears.
Beneath the clothesline
I had worn a path,
having been tempted at either end
by cars and cats and other dogs
and curious children,
one of whom I had bitten.
Father tossed me a bone,
said he'd see by Christ
how long I could live in a doghouse
before I changed my little tune.

I hung on,
and then some,
inhaling the hair and the clusters
and the bad breath of the dog
that had sacrificed his home:
until in the middle
of the third night
I called out to return.

In front of Franklin's crib
I swallowed a growl
to say I'd never say it again.
And I curled my fists that night
like Franklin's,
asleep in the bother
and the wonder
of a small skin.

TED KOOSER

Yevtushenko

Yevtushenko, you came to Nebraska.
Yes, of all places, Nebraska—
cornfield, wheatfield, cow and college.

You had a sore throat and you smelled of camphor.
Your blue eyes were small in your face.

You read your windy poems, Yevtushenko,
like a tree in the wind you read them,
waving your branches. We sat back
as far in our seats as we could,
frightened of Russia. Then it was over
and you scooped up your leaves and sat down.

After the party, we drove across town
to the Governor's house. It was already late.
You wanted to sit in the Governor's chair
and he let you. You drank his red wine
and showed us the long movie you'd made

of your life. You recited a list of the people
you knew: Kissinger, Nixon, Kennedy (Bob).

The Governor's eyes were as hollow as Lincoln's.
He nodded as Lincoln must have nodded
while Mary Todd Lincoln went over the menu.
At three in the morning, we finally left,
and when you thanked him, Yevtushenko, for his time,
he said it was all part of the job.

GREG KUZMA

Police

The police arrived early; I woke and heard
their motor running.
I was up before he was out of the car.
I was dressed before he was fully up the sidewalk
to the house.
I had descended the stairs just as his fist
hit the door.
I opened the door full upon him
shaking the last disheveled hair down.
I tried to appear indifferent, as if I had
been up for hours,
as if I had been myself on the job all night,
as if I knew already what it was he would say,
and that I perfectly understood
and forgave him entirely.
"We have one of your dogs in the trap this morning,"
he said, "And I must issue you another citation."
"Yes, I'm sorry about that," I said,

"She slipped away last night.
I was going to call you but I thought she would come
    back."
I was lying, really, I had not known
any of the dogs had left,
but this had happened so often I expected it.
It was part of living in Crete, Nebraska.
I think the police liked picking the dogs up.
It gave them a chance to ride in the car with a dog.
Otherwise they are not allowed.
Riding with a dog can be quite a pleasure.
I have often done it myself.

BRAD LEITHAUSER

A Michigan Ghosttown

It's as though even the ghosts
Have left: no sense of anyone
Lingering here; nothing to weight
The hundreds of poplars—locally
"Popple"—flickering in the light
Breezing of this cool Superior
Noon. Had I not been told
Where to pick out the vined
Roots of a settlement, I might
Have seen no trace at all.
                    It was nothing
But a boomtown, a roof
And a drink, built to last
As long as the timber did, which
Wasn't long. Yet the buzzsaws spun

Mounds and mounds of gold
Dust before they were done.

Up here, back then, it was boom-and-bust;
And after the bust
Sixty, seventy years of thin
Northern sun, of fog turning to snow,
And a tentative, tendrilous
Scrapping with rock and ice,
A re-routing of roots,
A noiseless supplanting as
The popple moved back in—

Trees take the streets.

JO McDOUGALL

Edge of America

In Kansas City, I'm shopping
the Sharper Image.
They've got the ocean on tape.
I step back ten years
to Maine, Mt. Desert Island, Thunder Hole
where, if you stand too close,
the ocean rages through a needle
and pulls thunder through your spine.
We hold each other, deaf and terrified.
Alone, safe and not far
from the exact center of the United States,
I think of the edge of America,
the gulls screaming around us like burning cats.

Story

Decades ago
in a small, mad town,
there is an evangelist, soon to be my father,
with black, brilliantined hair.
Standing before the borrowed pulpit, shoes buried in
    sawdust,
he marries my mother with his eyes.
He leaves her before I am born,
taking his Bible with him
and her mother's brooch.

My daughters love the story.
At five and seven they are already turned
toward someplace else,
they and others like them raised in towns
of summer revivals, visiting preachers,
the one wide highway out.

A Bottomlands Farmer Suffers a Sea Change

A man fits a key into the door of an office in Chicago.
Suddenly he remembers a plowed field.
He remembers the farm
before they took it.
He remembers walking its ditches,
flushing birds.

In a park across the street
pigeons scatter.
He hurries into the office
where a phone is ringing.

TODD MOORE

after work

i'd stop off at kenny's
funhouse it was a pie
shaped joint next to
the northwestern switch
tracks kenny used to
have bowls of crackers
& cheese & a big jug
of herring laid out on
the bar after being
around hot machines all
day cold beer slid
down easy & so what
if kenny had the pin
ball machines rigged i
liked the sound of bells
going off & the blinking
red & green numbers i
used to pretend i could
beat the system never
did kenny's main feature
was the chili it had
bullet sized peppers
floating around w/the
meat once when a guy
reached for a pepper
shaker kenny sd rape my
wife but don't fuck
w/the chili

HOWARD NEMEROV

Landscape with Self-Portrait

A shading porch, that's open to the west
Whence the weather comes, and giving on a lawn
Won from the meadow where the hay's been baled
In cubes like building blocks of dusty gold,
And further down, through trees, the streaming creek
With three still pools by passagework
Of rapids and rills in fretted rhythms linked;

And on the porch the life-defeated self
And reciprocating engine of reverie
Translating to time the back and forth of space,
The foot's escapement measuring the mind
In memories while the whole antic machine
Precesses across the floor and towards the edge
And has to be hitched back from time to time;

And there to watch the tarnished silver cloud
Advancing up the valley on a wind
That shudders the leaves and turns them silverside
While shadows sweep over stubble and grass,
And sudden the heavy silver of the first
Raindrops blown slanting in and summer cold
And turning continuous in silver strings;

And after that, the clarified serene
Of the little of daylight that remains to make
Distinct the details of the fading sight:
The laddered blue on blue of the bluejay's tail,
The sweeping swallows low above the swale
Among the insect victims as they rise
To be picked off, and peace is satisfied.

DUANE NIATUM

from *Warrior Artists of the Southern Plains*

I. Prisoners at Fort Marion: 1875–1878

When Cheyennes, Kiowas, and a Caddo step
through the door in double leg-irons,
without a trial or a hearing,
not one guard meets their eyes.

The door weighs on their shoulders
like a pendant of the long train journey.
From the farthest reaches of the fort

they watch for the one who will bring
them the key to sunrise.
The door remains shut.

They sit like sagebrush until only
their breaths and ribs show exile.
Almost every dawn or sunset they hear

the Sun Dance drums and taste the ashes
of Black Kettle's village at Sand Creek.
But they find a secret way home

in the pads given them by Captain Pratt
by drawing the ponies captured
from a Crow camp when the wind

followed their moccasins across
bear mountains and coyote bluffs.
Like their sky brother, Tornado, they

pull the door through Eagle's eye;
four quick strokes and it's a Sun Dance lodge;
two more and it's the sacred pipe woman.

The guards grow bored and multiply like blue
flies on the tin plates piled with food
a few Dog Soldiers ignore.

They strike hunger like a diamondback
as a bone-whistle welcomes geese above Red River.
If they can't challenge despair, its riddle

of air, these warriors will, at least, refuse
to utter to their conquerors what's
older and deadlier than grief.

III. Howling Wolf (1850–1927) Cheyenne

You dig your way beyond the domestic stone
of St. Augustine through a dream,
the dawn you and your brothers raided
a Pawnee camp for horses;
their manes glistened like open
questions near Flint river.

You will never carry your lance
or race this free again
on the trails of buffalo hunters.
But you will lead
the Bowstring Soldiers in a horse
dance honoring Chief Eagle Head's death,
your father. Shield, your mother, keens
of such a snare of grief
that no child clutches her blanket,
recognizes what has ruptured the blood.
She quit telling the story of how

the rainbow reflects the spirit
of your people's Medicine Lodge.
She tells no more stories
of the cottonwood leaves dangling in the wind
as if the earth pounded a drum for your dead.

You painted these scenes
because the Great Plains held you
until the path to the grey-fox sky
fell away like a cliff.
When the white man's car you were in
rolled upside down into a ditch,
killing you before the morning birds
stopped drinking in the light,
it is said, an eagle's scream echoed
from Lost Valley to Medicine Bluff
and on to Big Timbers, mapping your last
escape route one step before the prairie fire.

KURT NIMMO

All the Women in Suburbia

It was
Saturday
& I got in my car & I drove
around suburbia looking for women.
I didn't know where the women were hiding
I couldn't understand it—where were those
women just like me looking for somebody to love
or at least have noncommittal sex with
& I decided that the world is a terrible place

& it was all the fault of rich people
& church leaders & rabbis & government bureaucrats
everybody but myself because
I didn't have any influence
in the single bar scene.
I drove around
stopping at traffic signals
& searching up & down the clean sober streets
& inside the few cars around me for that
special woman with needs like my very own.
I drove my car
until suburbia gave away to the city
& the streets narrowed & grew dirty with
garbage & winos & hookers & broken-down cars
driven by insane people on cheap illegal drugs.
I knew that this wasn't the place
to find my girl
the girl of my dreams
wet or otherwise
& I decided to stop at a bar
& I did stop at a bar & inside the bar
& fat woman danced on a stage & her tits
were lethal weapons & she stared at me
with vicious stupid green eyes
& I thought about all the illegitimate children
in the world & government mandated sterilization
for unwed or retarded mothers
& I drank my beer & then I went home
& I crawled into bed & I stared at the grubby wall
& I thought about all the lonely women
out there in suburbia
washing between their legs
with clean pink wash-
cloths & drinking
champagne straight
out of the
bottle.

KATHLEEN NORRIS

Pommes de Terre

Three women laugh aloud
in a sun-dappled kitchen
in 1927, in South Dakota.
They are learning French
to improve themselves.

Twice a week they come together:
today, they are naming everything on the table.
"Haricots verts," one reads aloud,
pointing to the beans. "Green," says Elsa,
the German picture-bride,
lamenting the forests
she will never see again.
Lottie and Myrtle
recall a paradise of their own,
the gentle hills at Sioux City,
on down along the river.

They laugh in the afternoon
in a house set down
on a God-forsaken, near-treeless plain.
Each tree they planted in town
either broke with ice
or wilted in the rainless summer.

"Chou-fleur," they say,
for cauliflower. Potatoes
are "pommes de terre."
The words have such a soothing sound
Lottie repeats them
like a mother
comforting a child.

Oh, my earth apples:
my little pommes de terre,
my cabbage flowers,
oh yes: and now
the womens' cheeks and breasts are blooming,
their bottoms grow round
in the chintz dresses.
They are ladies, yes,
pious and respectable,
but they are laughing now,
beyond caring.

Such elegant potatoes:
pommes de terre, my dear,
oh my dears, oh yes.

At Anfinson's in Hettinger, North Dakota

They're in the hardware store
in a bad spring.
No rain last fall, bare fields all winter.
So far all the winds have stirred up
is topsoil, real estate changing hands.

Some say it's too dry to plant,
some say you can't afford not to.
It's all in their faces:
his beefy, apoplectic;
hers thin and worn.

They've loaded up a new ball hitch
and overalls.
He prices a new pump

and digs his hands deeper in his pockets.
Now she's walking slowly
down the long line of boots,
her eyes confused
as a newborn calf's.
"Everything's so high," she says aloud,
to herself.

He sits down
on a folding chair.
She's holding a boot,
holding it close, thinking
    egg money, spring butchers to sell
    later on,
    how long will that sole stitching
    hold?

"Don't they have my size?" he hollers
and she says absently,
"Do you want me to find them?"
"Well, whaddya think I brought you to town for, woman,
to look at you?"

RICHARD PFLUM

Putting It Somewhere

Let's put it anywhere but here.
Let's dump it in Indiana
or in Utah, put it under the lake
where no one will find it.
Let's dump it in Vermont or Maine,

THE MIDWEST

or in Montana or Washington State
under a mountain where earthquakes
maybe won't shake it loose;
or on the bottom of the sea
where the fish might love it, grow
corpulent, maybe sprout three heads
and sharp teeth.
Or on the sun, let's shoot it to the sun.
Hope the sun will enjoy it
or be too far away to spit it back
if the taste is really bad.

Let's give it to Canada wrapped up
in green ribbons like a gift; they certainly
have space in which to put it, or maybe
to Mexico wrapped in corn-shuck disguised
as tamales . . . so hot and so tangy.
I'm sure we can put it somewhere.
We have clever people who have studied
in universities; they understand
its strange light and unearthly warmth.
They have given the information
to important men in ties and white shirts
who make green money and give us jobs
and hospitals, who send out employees
in huge trucks to pick up our trash
every Thursday morning.
They will know what to do with it;
they deal with it all the time.
They have machines where it comes out
one end while fresh dollars in very
large denominations come out the other.
They are very clever people.

Today it is up to our ankles;
tomorrow it will be up to our knees.

We can feel it itching inside our socks,
squishing between reddened toes.
We were given dominion over it,
there must be a place to put it.
God must have provided a place.
Maybe in your backyard,
certainly not mine.

FRANK POLITE

In My Black Book

1

The fresh water goddess, Lake Erie,
is dead.

Every day now, more and more of her putrid corpse
washes up on the sand.

Fish that silvered in her veins, upturned and bloated.
Underwater plants she patiently tended,
mutant and withered.

Her foaming brains are deposited in Cleveland.
In banks. In Coke bottles.

2

I hate to say "I remember when" but I do.

I remember when swimming in her was like crystal-gazing.
I remember the autumn afternoon I made my first
deep dive as a child

and lost my bathing suit. Down, down in slow-motion
descent, naked, wide-eyed in the wavering
light, ringing in my ears . . .

I could see clear through
the shimmer of her blue-white veils down to the bottom,
her glowing shells, her lake stones like jewels.

And I was held, suspended, in the dance of a goddess.

3

Erie, it's no use.
You slump in thick and listless, like goulash soup.
Scientists say it will take at least
500,000 years before you regenerate, if you do . . .

O Erie, what are we going to do with you?

We have roped off our old approaches and posted warn-
    ings:
SEVERE POLLUTION ZONE, NO BATHING PERMITTED,
KEEP AT A SAFE DISTANCE.

We have dismantled our carousels and prancing horses.

And all along your shores
lanterns burn down to a low uneven glow
and go out.

In darkness, in silence
you lay out there a great snake goddess
dying, dead.

And each dawn, you coil the oily slime of our horizon.

4

Look, I still keep your address here
in my black book:

> Lake Goddess Erie
> c/o U.S.A.
> Western Hemisphere

RICHARD ROBBINS

The Change to One-Way after Repaving

The new road unfolds from the heart of downtown,
leaves the river, hurries past our house and oak
shade, on up to the flats and a hundred miles

of corn. Never again will we know so
keenly the momentum of commerce: Jim Grady speeds,
through fog even, to dimly lit interviews,

grower by grower, about futures. The sun
barely high enough to burn, office workers jog
toward inspiring rural miles

before returning to coffee, bites of toast.
This change of way reforms even us:
Our hearing fixes on that strange new hum of tires,

on their going away from everything
solid. Past the hidden prairie lakes, that hum
moves over the countryside, away, away,

well past the finite hope of any driver,
long since at home in the kitchen chair
on Meadow Court, breaking

bread among the singular faces of love.

Vandal

The kid who wrote *fuck* everywhere kissed his mom
and wore jeans frayed just right, not severely,
and once or twice a day stuck his face
into his Airedale's muzzle, rubbing noses. At night,

moon or no moon, he walked through Buck Park,
past Griffey's Cards and Gifts, to the shore.
He painted *fuck* on a riverside bench,
red *fuck* on an oak thick as his dad's car.

The water swept by. Lonely still,
he called an owl down, owl that didn't come,
and from behind the far hill he dreamed a great blue
heron angling that way and lowering,

and he wrote *fuck* on that. It hurt when he sprayed
that huge misty circle around his shoes.
He cried and cried. Then he was soft, then cold,
all without tearing himself apart.

LEN ROBERTS

Ten Below

Ten below and I followed my mother
in her patch-quilt bathrobe down Remsen
   and Ontario,
under the Black Bridge encased in ice, past
   Freihofer's stables
where the horses' breath rose to steam
   the dim yellow windows. Miles
she strode, calling out the name of her brother
who had played amateur baseball before Korea,
her sister with one leg gone,
snow now falling on her shoulders, turning
   her rollered hair white.
Stretching my legs to step in her prints,
I held back at corners when she stopped to curse
the red doors of the closed church,
the neon bull glowing from Boney's Bar.
An old couple walked by, their eyes lowered,
a car with chains rattled on the cobblestones,
but my mother was already gone
across the railroad tracks, to the island
and Little League field where she squatted
and yanked the pad out, let her blood
drop into the snow, small dark holes
I could barely see from the dugout
   less than twenty feet away.
Then she began yelling the names again
and I knew I would have to run soon
   for my father,
but in those ten degrees below zero
   I could not move, could

THE MIDWEST

only listen as I hardened
in the wind and snow, tightened,
drew into myself until I could not feel
my feet, my hands or face, and my breath
barely steamed the iron-cold air where
    my mother lay.

HERBERT SCOTT

Morning, Milking

In the cold barn before sunrise
the throaty speech of cows,
muzzles muffled in oats,
long-lashed haughty eyes.
I crouch on the small stool,
lean my forehead into the warm flank
of Scarlett, take hold
of the warty teats, while you,
Grandmother, a kerchief round
your hair, sing Kemo Kimo
to the dance of cats.

Now you leave the barn,
harnessed to milk, a foamy
pail at each side. Oh, the cows
are emptied of milk, the morning
milk, mouths aslant
the cows are chewing their cuds,
the cows are dreaming,

their languid, eclipsed eyes.
And you are walking the path
to the house where you will lift
cream for the churn thick
as egg custard in your hands.
You walk away from the sunrise,
beneath the mulberry trees, beneath
the windmill tangled
in honeysuckle, and I follow,
knuckles white, carrying
in either hand what I have taken.

LUCIEN STRYK

Luck—1932

After the market crash, everyone
short on luck, I squinted out
my bedroom window for the last time,

holding the rabbit's foot I'd
swopped my slingshot for, counted
numbers for a miracle that wouldn't

come. As the last mock-orange
petal in Andrade's yard spun into
summer, the junkman divvied up

our table, chairs, beds, all we
could not cart off from Chicago, for
a piddling sum. Clutching my can

of marbles, baseball mitt, I followed
mother lugging my baby sister,
worldly goods stuffed in a canvas

bag. Tracking my father, job to
job, St. Louis to Columbus. All
that year I made spells, counting

heads, trees, fireflies, polished my
wishbone seven times, again. Until
I landed back in the old city,

raced to Washington Park, joined my
playmates, Shorty, Tonsils, Mike,
riding Taft's human pyramic of *Time.*

As I explained how luck had brought
us back, I found real magic, twigs
sparkling into flower before my eyes.

WILLIAM TROWBRIDGE

Late Fall Night

Alone on our porch swing, I hear the Future
Farmers gun their pickups around the square,
squealing tires, blaring horns, bleating
trucker love in quadrophonic, neolithic
stereo. The chilly midnight air smells
faintly of packing house and hydrocarbons.
From behind our garage, the neighbor's ring-tailed
tom yowls his urges. Later he'll respray

our front door for his pack of floozies. Even
the crickets, their green ship listing hard
to winter, play it hot as gypsies on a binge.

Above this din, waves and waves of snow geese,
bellies lighted by the town, spread out
in u's and v's and w's, calling up
and down the ranks. I watch as the calls
die out and the bellies disappear south
beyond the power plant. Our mantel clock
bongs the half hour. Addled, I try a plea:
"Take me with you!" "This is not my home," I lie.
Grounded on cats and crickets, pickups fueled
on lovers' nuts, I stand for our raunchy anthem,
full enough to steal a bike and pump
no-handed clear around the courthouse.

MONA VAN DUYN

In the Missouri Ozarks

Under an overwashed, stiff, gray
sheet of sky, the hills
lie like a litter of woodchucks,
their backs mottled black with leafless
branches and brown with oakleaves,
hanging on till spring.
Little towns are scabs in their haunches.

Out of the hills the pickups scuttle
like water beetles onto the highway,
which offers up STUCKEY'S, EATS,

GOD'S WELL, CAVES,
JUNQUE, HOT BISCUITS 'N'
CREAM GRAVY, $6. OVERNIGHT
CABINS and a WINERY
to the chilled traveller.

Town leads off with a garish motel,
followed by the Shopping Plaza—
a monster of a supermarket
and a few frail shops; then comes
the courthouse square, with a barnfaced
Dollar Department Store,
Happy's Hardware and TV,
Shorty's Beer-Cafe,
two quiet banks and a chiropractor.
Big white gingerbreaded houses
and new ranchstyles
fizzle out on the edge of town
to yellow, brickpatterned tarpaper
shacks, leaning against the firewood
stacked as high as their roofs.

Off the highway, frosty weeds
lift berries and pods
on either side of the road in a mileslong
wine and black and beige bouquet,
and every twenty acres or so
a fieldstone cottage
guards its pastured cows
and its woods of oak and black walnut.
Farm dogs explode from porches
and harry the car down the gravel,
yipping at stones spat from the wheels.
Out here, after the supper dishes,
three or four couples will walk down the road
to a neighbor's, and will sit

around the heating stove,
talking about Emma Harbis,
who is finally giving away cuttings
of her famous orange-blooming
Kalanchoë, and about the Ed Lelands,
on food stamps all year,
but with a brand new pickup
parked bold as brass
in their front yard, and about
Old Lady Kerner, who was seen
in the drugstore buying Oil of Olay
to smooth out the wrinkles
eighty-two hard years have hammered
into her indomitable face.

MARK VINZ

Roadside Attraction

You can tell right off what's happening
from the fresh pine boards across the windows.
Even the old gas pump is gone,
sold last week to a man who owns a restaurant—
thinks he'll make a big fishbowl out of it.
It'll be cute, he says, a real attention getter
when you walk in the front door.

Wouldn't you know, somebody stopped for gas
the very next day, lost from the Interstate.
We sold him some chewing gum
and then he looked kind of sad.

Real interesting place you've got here,
he said, I'll have to stop again
sometime I'm passing through.

Nothing much left inside now—
just some shoelaces and lamp wicks,
the canned goods that never sold.
Maybe we should turn the place into a bar—
drive to Fargo and get back that gas pump.
A real attention getter is what the man said.
We could use one of those.

DIANE WAKOSKI

The Ring of Irony

What do you say to the mother
of a homosexual man
whom you once were married to,
when she asks you to return your wedding ring
because it's a family heirloom?
    "I want to keep it on my key ring
    where I carry it now,
    to remind me of loss?"
or perhaps, in spite,
    "It was the only thing
    I ever got out of the marriage.
    No. I won't give it back."
Do you say that you love irony
and have imagined your whole life
governed by understatement

and paradox?
Yet, the obvious dominates and
I ask myself,
"Why do you want to keep it?
Surely the woman deserves some comfort/
if a small piece of gold can do it,
who can object?"
Wallowing again, in the obvious,
I wonder at my meanness,
my own petty anger
at men who love other men,
alas, some of them are/ have been
my best friends. Irony?
No. The obvious.
Why do you want that circle of gold
lying in your purse with keys
and checkbooks? I nudge myself.
Why don't you purchase an ounce of gold
and carry it in a velvet bag instead. Your
own.
Worth so much more.
Of course. The obvious.
Because the other was given,
not bought, and you
have never asked the return of your gifts, but
you know, Diane, why
you anguish over putting the ring in the box and
mailing it off to
Corona, California.
So obvious.
Because you believe in the gifts
freely given
to appease destiny.
You too would sacrifice
Iphigenia or Isaac
for the cap of darkness,

having given your children
for poetry,
having given your sexuality
for beautiful men,
having relinquished honor
for music.
The circle of gold,
that ring, symbolizes
the pact.
To give it back says the giving was meaningless.
Fate does not honor your bargain,
Ms. Wakoski. Not irony,
the obvious:
you have no husband,
      no house,
      no children,
      no country.
You have no fame,
        fortune,
only remaindered books,
and innocent students who
stab you
with their lack of understanding,
asking, no not ironically,
"Did you give a lot of readings
when you were young?"
Finally, the understatement, the irony, when I say,
"yes," and the past swallows up everything,
leaving the obvious,
and now that handsome woman in California
wants to take the ring.

Soap opera of the middle-aged
mid-Western
schoolteacher?
What do you say when irony deserts you

for the maudlin obvious?
"I am mailing you the ring.
Your claim is greater than mine."

Irony? No, the obvious.

DAVID WOJAHN

Heaven for Railroad Men

You're still a young man,
he says, not to his son,
it's his bitterness he's
talking to and
at the restaurant
he orders a fourth round
before dinner.
With Mother wiping
her glasses at the table,

I help him from his chair
to the john. He pees slowly,
fingers like hams
on his fly, a complex
test of logic
for a man this drunk.
I'm splashing cold water in his face

and he tells me he's dying,
Don't say a thing to your Mother,
and please, Dave,
don't ever remember me like this.

I remember how you said you
needed to ride
the baggage cars forever,
passing prairie towns
where silos squat like
pepper shakers on dry earth.
I want to be six again
and sway with you
down the sagging rails
to Minot, Winnipeg, and beyond,
your mailsacks piled
like foothills of the Rockies.

You're unloading your government Colt,
unzipping your suitcase
for Canadian inspectors.
Father, when I touched you
I was trembling.

Heaven for railroad men
begins with a collapsed trestle.
The engine goes steaming
off into nothing.
There are no rails to hold you.
You're singing country-western
at the top of your lungs.
You go flying forever,
the door pulled open,
mailsacks scattered
into space like seed.

ELIZABETH WOOD

Christmas Mass

My graduation mass
was the last time
I went to church
until now—twenty years

I remember grandma's
tears that day
the priest took me
to St. Paul Mission School

The nuns told me
my soul was black
and beat my hands
for going to Wacipi

They told me
I must confess my sins
My cousin told me
to make some up

I learned to say
I lied ten times
since my last confession
Father forgive me

I never chewed the wafers
they laid on my tongue
Christ's body they told me
I never understood

They told me Christ
came to save Indians too
Lonesome for grandma
I didn't feel saved

Now the tabernacle
is a doe-skin teepee
painted with four colors
One for each direction

The priest says Christ
is like a circle
a medicine wheel

no beginning—no end
He is wakan—I am wakan
Now I understand

The staff
in Jesus' hand
trails ribbons
like the sundance pole

NEW YORK CITY

JACK ANDERSON

from *Field Trips on the Rapid Transit*

You have come so far you can imagine nothing further.
But here is where you can change to go still further on.

A whole tree of stations grows from the subway here
Affording shelter and shade like any tree on a hill.

Deep in the roots of BROADWAY–EAST NEW YORK station
You feel slow as a worm, you can't seem to get moving.

The platform looks longer than the ride to Far Rockaway.
But then there are steps and a pale light—and it's day-
    light.

Escalators ascend the trunk of this tree
And you're already above the trees outside.

You're up at the top where the el lines branch
Above you, below you, on all sides with their tracks:

Platforms over platforms, stations over stations
Shaking in the wind as the trains pass like seasons,

And tracks reaching upward, tracks twisting down around,
But always branching, branching out from this place, and

Everything moving now, moving to a different place,
Yet everything joined, a part of one system,

As you, too, are part of it as you make your connection
And continue onward to the end of this line.

JOHN CEELY

Heart Beats the Rent Collector

I wrestle this skinny Afro Puerto Rican. Summon
strength to tip him off balance. Third man I've
fought on my collection rounds tonight. It comes
to equilibrium. Twist them off balance, they pay.

(We are in a series of crisscross hallways thru my
buildings running side to side as well as front to
back: so I entered at Avenue A & can stay inside
till Avenue C.)

This slender man my size & weight—light-coffee
colored, hip jokester—they say he digs to kill
"with heart." I've bent him nearly off balance
when he begins to let his power rise. I pushed
him too hard too soon. Slowly back to vertical,
he's whispering, "Friend, there ain't but one way
to kill. You use heart & you work slow. You
raise your heart on top of your man's heart & your
heart is the size of his. Dig: both are pulsing
vessels. I push down my heart so it enters my
man's heart, it fits easy. I have slid inside
from above. My man is dead."

AMY CLAMPITT

The Subway Singer

Survivor and unwitting
public figure—a gaunter one
since with her cane, accordion
and cup, I last saw her

tap her hard way along
the hurled col, with its serial
crevasses, of an IRT train,
and heard the cracked bell

of her battered alto rung
again above the grope and jostle,
the knee-jerk compunction
of the herd at the faint signal

it's all but past hearing,
from beyond the ashen
headland, the mist-shrouded
hollows of her lifted

sightlessness—seen waiting
now on the platform, as it were
between appearances, a public figure
shrunken but still recognizable,

she links in one unwitting
community how many who have heard
and re-heard that offering's fall
toward the poorbox of oblivion?

IRA COHEN

Tip the Light Fantastic

for Timothy Baum

Talking to Timothy on the telephone
is like taking in 50 years of French cinema
in fifteen minutes
Homage to the man in the white suit
& to those upper East side thriftshops
You mimic a decade of genius in a single
squeal while spooning diaphragm jelly
into the mouth of the Park Avenue Princess
Your hobby horse is rocking all night
on 29th and Lexington
It's three A.M. & your man is out of town
It doesn't really matter though
since Max Ernst, Tristan Tzara & Man Ray
are waiting for you to come home
Remember the fireworks over the Battery,
her ass was not even beautiful,
yet it was there to be forgotten by Huelsenbeck
I wanted to record a single vignette—
O yes, as you were saying, it was Gerard's
21st birthday & you gave him a tuxedo
which he wore with a pair of motorcycle boots
when he went w/ Warhol to a chic party
for Salvador Dali—What a camp!
He gave his name as Count Gerardo *Melonga*
& you watched as Dali leaned over to kiss
his hand saying softly, "I knew your father
very well."
Dear Timothy, may yr next doubleheader be a winner
I give you, just this once, tomorrow's newspaper
today & return yr toast vintage for vintage
Faire la cour toujours!

CORNELIUS EADY

Atomic Prayer

If the bomb drops
And I'm riding the
Staten Island Ferry,
Give me time to spit in the water.
If the bomb drops
And I'm on top
Of the Empire State Building,
Give me time
To toss a penny
Off the observation deck.
If the bomb drops
And I'm approaching the subway,
Let me have the chance
To jump the turnstile.
If the bomb drops
And I'm walking down Fifth Ave.,
Grant me a loose brick,
A fresh plate glass window.
Grant us a moment
When there'll be no need
To play it safe.
Give to us the pleasure
Of misdemeanors.
Let each of us do
What we've always
Dreamed of,
But were too polite
To act out.
Let us extract
Our brief revenge,
Spilling and ripping things

We've been taught
Not to handle.
If we're to die before we sleep,
Grant us a moment to uncover
The secrets behind the door marked RESTRICTED,
Authorize us to touch what was always held
          just beyond our reach.
Give us a taste
Of the stolen world.

EDWARD FIELD

The Last Bohemians

for Rosetta Reitz

We meet in a cheap diner and I think, God,
the continuity, I mean, imagine
our still being here together
from the old days of the Village
when you had the bookshop on Greenwich Avenue
and Jimmy Baldwin and Jimmy Merrill used to drop in.
Toying with your gooey chicken, you remind me
how disappointed I was with you for moving
to Eighth Street and adding gifts and art cards,
but little magazines, you explain, couldn't pay the rent.
Don't apologize, I want to say, it's been forty years!

Neither of us, without clinging to our old apartments,
could pay Village rents nowadays,
where nobody comes "to be an artist" anymore.
Living marginally still, we are shabby as ever,
though shabby was attractive on us once—those years

when the latest Williams or Stevens or Moore was sold
in maybe five bookstores, and the Horton
biography of Hart Crane an impossible find.
Continuity! We're still talking of our problems
with writing, finding a publisher,
as though that was the most important thing in the
        world—
sweetheart, we are as out of it as old lefties.

Someone came into my apartment recently and
        exclaimed,
"Why, it's bohemian!" as if she had discovered the last
of a near-extinct breed. Lady, I wanted to protest,
I don't have clamshell ashtrays, or chianti bottles
encrusted with candle wax, or Wilhelm Reich,
Henry Miller and D. H. Lawrence,
much less Kahlil Gibran and Havelock Ellis,
on my bricks-and-boards bookshelves.
But it's not just the Salvation Army junk she saw,
or the mattress and pillows on the floor—
my living style represented for her the aesthetic
of an earlier generation, the economics, even,
of a time, our time, Rosetta, before she was born.

The youth still come weekends, though not to "see
a drag show," or "bull daggers fighting in the gutters,"
or to "pick up a queer or artist's model."
But there is something expectant in them
for something supposed to be here, once called,
(shiver) bohemian. Now it's I who shiver
as I pass them, fearing their rage against
an old guy with the sad face of a loser.
Daytime, it's safer, with couples in from the suburbs
browsing the antique shops.
I find it all so boring, but am stuck here,
a ghost in a haunted house.

At a movie about a war criminal whose American
lawyer daughter blindly defends him—blasted by the
    critics
because it is serious and has a message—
the audience is full of old Villagers, drawn to see it
because it's serious and has a message,
the women, no longer in dirndles and sandals,
but with something telltale about the handcrafted jewelry,
the men not in berets, but the kind that would wear
    them—
couples for whom being young meant being radical,
meant free love. Anyway,
something about them says Villager,
maybe the remnants of intellect, idealism—
which has begun to look odd on American faces.

Nowadays, there's nothing radical left, certainly not
in the Village, no Left Bank to flee to, no justification
for artistic poverty, nothing for the young to believe in,
except their careers, and the fun of flaunting
their youth and freaky hairstyles in trendy enclaves.

Leftovers from the old Village, we spot each other
drifting through the ghostly
high rental picturesque streets, ears echoing
with typewriters clacking and scales and arpeggios
heard no more, and meet fugitive in coffee shops,
partly out of friendship, but also, as we get shabbier and
    rarer,
from a sense of continuity—like, hey, we're historic!—
and an appreciation, even if we never quite got there,
of what our generation set out to do.

ALLEN GINSBERG

Velocity of Money

for Lee Berton

I'm delighted by the velocity of money as it whistles
    through windows of Lower East Side
Delighted by skyscrapers rising old grungy apartments
    falling on 84th pavement
Delighted by inflation that drives me out on the street
After all what good's the family farm, why eat turkey by
    millions every Thanksgiving
Why not Star Wars? Why the same old America?!?
George Washington wasn't good enough! Tom Paine,
    pain in the neck, Whitman a jerk!
Delighted by double digit interest rates in Capitalist worlds
I always was Communist, now we'll win
as usury makes walls thinner, books thicker & dumber
Usury makes my poetry more valuable
my manuscripts worth their weight in useless gold—
Now everybody's atheist like me, nothing's sacred
buy and sell your grandmother, eat up old age homes,
Peddle babies on the street, pretty boys for sale on Times
    Square with crack spasms—
Burn down Amazonas, stink bomb heaven sulphuric, sar-
    coma plutonic Oregon, garbage dump Sargasso
You can shoot brown heroin, narcs sniff white cocaine,
Homeless benches, plastic huts, Africans sleep in
    Tompkins Park forever!
Macho men can fite on the Nicaraguan border and get
    paid with paper!
The velocity's what counts as the National Debt gets
    higher
Everybody running after the rising dollar
Crowds of joggers down broadway past City Hall on the
    way to the Fed

NEW YORK CITY

Nobody reads Dostoyevsky books so they'll have to give
    passing ear
to my fragmented ravings in between President's speeches
Nothing's happening but the collapse of the Economy
so I can go back to sleep till the landlord wins his eviction
    suit in court.

                                    2/18/86—10 AM

ARTHUR GREGOR

Gentle Lamb

At a street corner
waiting to cross: two boys.
Pressed against the chest of one
a dog slender as a greyhound,
timid as a lamb.

Traffic is heavy,
the boys are waiting for
a path to form.
Here in midtown New York
on a gray winter day,

they are a vision dimmed
in most, are the dream
flowing through their eyes and skin—
fire on this frost-
and world-encrusted ground.

And like a flare
sustained and surrounded by air,
the dog enfolded by

the boy's arm
rests on a tenderness

the boy is himself
seeking to express,
a tenderness before which he—
also at home in
an invisible mantle

that clings to him,
gentle as a lamb—
is himself dumb
as the animal
he carries in his arm.

MARILYN HACKER

Runaways Café I

You hailed a cab outside the nondescript
yuppie bar on Lexington to go
downtown. Hug; hug: this time I brushed my lips
just across yours, and fire down below
in February flared. O bless and curse
what's waking up no wiser than it was.
I will not go to bed with you because
I want to very much. If that's perverse,
there are, you'll guess, perversions I'd prefer:
fill the lacunae in: one; two; three; four . . .
I did, cab gone. While my late bus didn't come,
desire ticked over like a metronome.
For you, someone was waiting up at home.
For me, I might dare more if someone were.

RUDY KIKEL

Mother (from *Autographs, 1955*)

". . . Just what effort you will make
you're the one to say.
One more step refuse to take,
where you stop you'll stay."

While some other immigrant
girls of your generation were
    going into the Ridgewood
knitting mills at half the pay—you

    could be met emerging from
an apartment on Central Park
    West nearly every two weeks
once—a *Majestic* maid's night out.

    After fourteen effortful
years, you were able to furnish
    the Astoria flat and,
later, help papa get started

    in business. But by then you
had gone into business yourself,
    facing a novel horror:
how does one justify spending

    all of one's time on garden
and home when they have become one's
    own? Women friends had the same
problem. So with them you could talk.

    Only husband had no ear
for what you had to say. Children

helped, because children were all
ears. You developed in mustard

    plaster, chicken soup, honey,
tea, and "Please excuse Rudy" notes
    some proficiency. I got
down valetudinarian

    skills that became a resource
in dealing with high school torments:
    compulsory athletics
and tough peers. Mother, as if out

    of some vast succouring sea,
I seem always to have heard you
    loud and clear. Can I have mis-
taken your meaning: "refuse . . . stay"?

DONALD LEV

The Human Condition in Brighton Beach

Did you see the salt shaker?
It has been carried away.
And the onion that lay in slices on this very table only
    yesterday
is likewise mysteriously vanished.
And the lace curtains that moved so gracefully in that
    window
are gone also.
And the porcelain pitcher from Mexico, I'd never think
    to miss it,
but I see it's not in its usual place on the book shelf.

What has happened to the independent clutter about me?
What tricks are occurring, and why?
There was a third left to that stick of butter only just a
    moment ago.
Where is it now?

It's not madness. I am sure of that. I am sure of that.
Madness is such an oldfashioned idea and it would never
    apply to me.
My friends would have told me by now. They hold noth-
    ing back from me.

I think I'd better go for a walk. I'll take an umbrella.
I'll walk over to the beach to have a look at the sea,
or I'll go up to Coney Island Avenue and buy a knish.
A kasha knish, maybe, with a cup of very light coffee.
Then I'll go to the post office and buy some stamps.
Just so I can stand on the line and grumble together
with everybody else and watch how the wily Russians
sneak to the front of the line. But what did I do with my
    key?

This is beginning to get to me. I can't leave the house
    without my key.
And obviously, if I stay here I'll go crazy.

STANLEY MOSS

Potato Song

Darkness, sunlight and a little holy spit
don't explain an onion with its rose windows
and presentiment of the sublime,

a green shoot growing out of rock,
or the endless farewells of trees.
Wild grasses don't grow just to feed sheep,
hold down the soil or keep stones from rolling,
they're meant to be seen, give joy, break the heart.
But potatoes hardly have a way of knowing.
They sense if it is raining or not,
how much sunlight or darkness they have,
not crows or red-winged blackbirds overhead.
They are almost unaware of the battles of worms,
the nightmares of moles, underground humpings.
Like soldiers in the field and the terribly poor,
they do not sleep or wonder. Sometimes
I hear them call me "mister" from the ditch.
Workers outside my window in Long Island
cut potatoes in pieces, bury them, water them.
Each part is likely to sprout and flower.
No one so lordly not to envy that.

SHARON OLDS

Summer Solstice, New York City

By the end of the longest day of the year he could not
    stand it,
he went up the iron stairs through the roof of the building
and over the soft, tarry surface
to the edge, put one leg over the complex green tin cor-
    nice
and said if they came a step closer that was it.
Then the huge machinery of the earth began to work for
    his life,

the cops came in their suits blue-grey as the sky on a
    cloudy evening,
and one put on a bullet-proof vest, a
black shell around his own life,
life of his children's father, in case
the man was armed, and one, slung with a
rope like the sign of his bounden duty,
came up out of a hole in the top of the neighboring
    building
like the gold hole they say is in the top of the head,
and began to lurk toward the man who wanted to die.
The tallest cop approached him directly,
softly, slowly, talking to him, talking, talking,
while the man's leg hung over the lip of the next world
and the crowd gathered in the street, silent, and the
hairy net with its implacable grid was
unfolded near the curb and spread out and
stretched as the sheet is prepared to receive at a birth.
Then they all came a little closer
where he squatted next to his death, his shirt
glowing its milky glow like something
growing in a dish at night in the dark in a lab and then
everything stopped
as his body jerked and he
stepped down from the parapet and went toward them
and they closed on him, I thought they were going to
beat him up, as a mother whose child has been
lost will scream at the child when it's found, they
took him by the arms and held him up and
leaned him against the wall of the chimney and the
tall cop lit a cigarette
in his own mouth, and gave it to him, and
then they all lit cigarettes, and the
red, glowing ends burned like the
tiny campfires we lit at night
back at the beginning of the world.

MOLLY PEACOCK

Subway Vespers

Thank you for some ventilation and free hands.
Thank you that the man with whiskey breath and
bloodshot eyes, business suit, plus monogrammed

cuffs (likely to behave) is significantly
taller than I am, leaving me inches of free
space between my place at the pole, his, and the lady

weeping below me. Over the loudspeaker a voice
informs us a track obstruction leaves no choice
but for a man to check each car's wheels twice.

Obstruction? Must be a body. Try to see:
nothing but black tunnel walls and the guilty
heads of those with seats. Thank you for my dusty
    clothes.

and that we are not naked in a cattle car.
After they find the body, we won't have to walk far.
A man's legs dangle above the door—

he's alive, mumbling into his beeper.
The conductor replies on the loudspeaker,
"Only garbage on the track!" You, our keeper,

we thank you for releasing the brake.
We'll go home, buyers of fish, bread, and steak,
to sit and watch the news we do not make.

The engine starts. We're head by head. No one's dead.
Then my prick of disappointment we weren't led
out of the car, past the body, down the track bed.

JAMES PURDY

The Brooklyn Branding Parlors

The Brooklyn branding parlors
are a temple of torture
their address changes nightly.
Young men go there to prove their manhood
the master of the place wears a mask
the exposed parts of his body
    appear to be stained with walnut juice
though perhaps he is black
his eyes alone are fairly visible
they shoot fire but don't look insane.
The penitent is tied to an iron halter
& chooses the instrument of his pain:
hot irons or the whip,
or if he thinks he is a hero, both.
Even though the sufferer is gagged
his screams of bloody murder
reach the outdoors.
Hence the parlors change their site nightly
like a wandering medicine show.
I wonder, do they exist?
If not, why do men go on talking about them?

Solitary in Brooklyn

Solitary hotel, I know you!
You have a ballroom
where boys of 15
dance under yellow globes
with men of 40.
None of the dancers are allowed to kiss

but close pressure slips by unnoticed.
When the dance hall closes
the boys depart with escorts,
and the 40-year-old men,
exhausted, footsore
slump down at tables where
coffee is served
by 25-year-old waiters
who were themselves once ballroom boys.
Drinking cup after cup of cappuccino
the men catch again whiffs of
the shampooed scalps and
woodsy armpits
of the dancing boys.

LYNNE SAVITT

I'm Glad You Are Casually Interested in Why I Was an Hour Late / or Take Your Fucking Hands Off My Throat

You were right my mountain of morality
             I have to admit
I was in Port Authority
             twirling tassled tits
For an audience of hundreds that
             happened to include
Four Hell's Angels
Two Black Panthers
Seven bums that were stewed.

             I did my show
                 leopard G string on

And when my audience
    was almost gone
My leather clad phantom
    took me away
On his beautiful lightning BSA
He was an expert
    knew what to do
We won a Silver Cup
    in the power shift screw

He beat me up
    and threw me out
Then I deflowered two priests
    and three boy scouts

    The cigarettes you found in
        the back seat
    Belong to three sailors
        I happened to eat
    Don't tell me, Darling,
        that it's crude
    You know I just adore seafood!

Isn't it amazing
    my energetic power?
I did those things
    in just one hour!

    You'd like to believe it
        my adorable mate
    Not that I dropped Chuck at the subway
        and class let out late

This is a love poem
    of sorts, my dear.
Because I am telling you
    what you wanted to hear.

JAMES SCHUYLER

This Dark Apartment

Coming from the deli
a block away today I
saw the UN building
shine and in all the
months and years I've
lived in this apartment
I took so you and I
would have a place to
meet I never noticed
that it was in my view.

I remember very well
the morning I walked in
and found you in bed
with X. He dressed
and left. You dressed
too. I said, "Stay
five minutes." You
did. You said, "That's
the way it is." It
was not much of a surprise.

Then X got on speed
and ripped off an
antique chest and an
air conditioner, etc.
After he was gone and
you had changed the
Segal lock, I asked
you on the phone, "Can't
you be content with

your wife and me?" "I'm
not built that way,"
you said. No surprise.

Now, without saying
why, you've let me go.
You don't return my
calls, who used to call
me almost every evening
when I lived in the coun-
try. "Hasn't he told you
why?" "No, and I doubt he
ever will." Goodbye. It's
mysterious and frustrating.

How I wish you would come
back! I could tell
you how, when I lived
on East 49th, first
with Frank and then with John,
we had a lovely view of
the UN building and the
Beekman Towers. They were
not my lovers, though.
You were. You said so.

BARBARA SORETSKY

Only Child

I still remember my child playing
on the Lower East Side. A car crushed his father
as he was running from the cops.

I wrapped my son in a blanket,
held him close, rocked him lovingly.
He never thanked me. Instead,
he curled up like a worm.

My child grew restless indoors,
bleached by yellow lightbulbs,
warmed by radiators. He crept under furniture
where he set small fires. I made excuses
for his mischief as I was putting out the flames.
I tore up his teacher's painful notes.
I kept him home.

When he grew older, I warned him,
"Don't breathe in your father's ghost!"
I couldn't stop him. Each night
he loaded his father's gun
and disappeared. He left me staring
at the naked women torn from magazines
and tacked to the wall over his bed.

I found empty wallets under his bed.
I found purses under piles of underwear.
I found watches, some still ticking.
I found rings, earrings, gold chains.

He was gone too long.
When he came home, the sun was climbing the walls.
The cops were silently crouching.
He reached for his gun. They clubbed him
with their nightsticks. They kicked him
in the stomach. He bent over
like a dead fetus. I cried,
"Don't take my only son!"
The cops dragged him to the precinct.
I was sorry he was born.
I should have kept him in my womb.

They returned my son's spirit in a small package.
I had to pay the postage. Like a fly,
he darted from room to room, banged into walls,
zigzagged under furniture. When I told him
that I would never again allow him to leave home,
he landed on a yellow lightbulb, became overheated.
He shrivelled up and fell to the floor.

DAVID TRINIDAD

Driving Back from New Haven

Tim looks at his watch, reaches into his
pocket, takes out a small plastic container
and swallows an AZT pill with a sip of Sprite.
"Poison," he mutters under his breath. I
glance over at him. We haven't talked about
his health the entire trip. "How does it
make you feel?" I ask "Like I want to live
until they discover a cure," he snaps. We
travel in silence for a while. I stare out
the window at all the green trees on the
Merritt Parkway. Then he says: "I resent
it. I resent that we were not raised with
an acceptance of death. And here it is,
all around us. And I fucking resent it.
I resent that we do not know how to die."

THE
NORTHEAST

ELIZABETH ALEXANDER

A Poem for Nelson Mandela

Here where I live it is Sunday.
From my room I hear black
children playing between houses
and the El at a Sabbath rattle.
I smell barbecue from every direction
and hear black hands tolling church bells,
hear wind hissing through elm trees
through dry grasses

        On a rooftop of a prison
in South Africa Nelson Mandela
tends garden and has a birthday,
as my Jamaican grandfather in Harlem, New York
raises tomatoes and turns ninety-one.
I have taken touch for granted: my grandfather's hands,
his shoulder, his pajamas which smell of vitamin pills.
I have taken a lover's touch for granted,
recall my lover's touch from this morning
as his wife pulls memories through years
and years

      My life is black and filled with fortune.
Nelson Mandela is with me because I believe
in symbols; symbols bear power; symbols demand
power; and that is how a nation
follows a man who leads from prison
and cannot speak to them. Nelson Mandela
is with me because I am a black girl
who honors her elders, who loves
her grandfather, who is a black daughter

as Mandela's daughters are black
daughters. This is Philadelphia
and I see this Sunday clean.

West Indian Primer

for Clifford L. Alexander, Sr. (1897–1989)

"On the road between Spanish-Town
and Kingston," my grandfather said,
"I was born." His father a merchant,
Jewish, from Italy or Spain.

In the great earthquake the ground split
clean, and great-grandfather fell
in the fault with his goat. I don't know
how I got this tale and do not ask.

His black mother taught my grand-
father figures, fixed codfish cakes
and fried plantains, drilled cleanliness,
telling the truth, punctuality.

"There is no man more honest,"
my father says. Years later
I read that Jews passed through my
grandfather's birthplace frequently.

I know more about Toussaint
and Hispaniola than my own
Jamaica and my family tales.
I finger the stores like genie

lamps. I write this West Indian primer.

AMIRI BARAKA

from *A Poem of Destiny*

New Ark Space
is forked
pitch
black Sun
at noon.

The people lay
       roll
       laid &
       stretched yet
           incompletely
               out!

Yet they are truly *out!*

Mostly Children
    of the
       Sun

Descendants of the Earth's
    1st Priests
    & Scientists

Try to dig through the concrete
    who 'em is
    & Yes from No

What is Good
    & Why
  The Madness?
      ◆

In New Ark

there's grey
    icicle
Santa Claus
    death
    bldg.

Lincoln there Fucked up
    in stone.

There's niggers who are completely
    Greasy Heads
    Words Greasy
    Heads inserted

    like pee pee smells
    just behind the
    vestibule

    Yet A Broad
Mother fuckers of all
    descriptions

    gentled by media lighting
the noise holds a framing silence

        Solo
        &
    Ensemble

We all rock w/ the ark
    & try to make our
    33 or 45
    degrees

Endarkened or
Dead!

Wit me A
is repeating
better to
see
than dream
better to dream
than
be dead!

ALAN CATLIN

Pushing Forty

It wasn't supposed to be this way:
pushing forty against a bar with no career
to speak of. It was supposed to be easier,
a job in the Arts, respect among peers,
a stipend or two maybe even a Grant.
But, of course, it didn't work out that way.
Dead end streets are hard to escape from and
I've been on one for years—just count the empties.
Not that they mean anything, I know guys with
great jobs who drink almost that much at lunch
and go back to work. Everyone tells me the 60's
was a great time to grow up in but what if you
still believe working for material success is a
drag, that being plugged in to The System

is just another cause you have to fight
and you want to but you still believe in
paying bills. The only thing that didn't suck
about the 60's was the music and a great year
for baseball in 69. Drugs claimed all kinds
of people, man, including my supplier dead
from exiting on an on-ramp at sixty miles
an hour on the Jersey Turnpike. I learned about
his funeral about a year too late not being
a full pledged Fraternity brother.
Last week, one of his brothers jumped into
a small man-made lake at Albany State
and got fried in a freak accident.
Brought back memories of college and life
in the fast lane. Did you see *The Big Chill?*
It opens with Kline giving his kid a bath singing
Jeremiah was a Bullfrog just before he learns
his best friend from college had committed suicide.
Reminded me, we were coming down out of a fog
North of Utica barrelling out of control toward
this construction everyone asleep including
the driver when The Three Dog Night arrived
on the radio to save the day. Twenty years later
we're still going downhill all the way only
in opposite directions. It's almost like
a game to see who hits the embankment first.

BILLY COLLINS

Lowell, Mass.

Kerouac was born in the same town
as my father, but my father never
had time to write *On the Road*

let alone drive around the country
in circles.

He wrote notes for the kitchen table
and a novel of checks
and a few speeches to lullaby
businessmen after a fat lunch

and some of his writing is within
me for I house catalogues of jokes
and handbooks of advice
on horses, snow tires, women,

along with some short stories
about the deadbeats at the office,
but he was quicker to pick up
a telephone than a pen.

Like Jack, he took a drink but
beatific to him meant the Virgin Mary.

He called jazz jungle music
and he would have told Neal Cassady
to let him off at the next light.

JOHN DeWITT

Old Post Grill

The OPG right on the state line
where the boys went on Friday nights
no dates at the Old Post Grill
and one night there was a club
there from Norwalk and some guys
from Westport and Danny Kinaly
grabs the mike and starts yelling
"Stamford is king. Stamford is king.
Norwalk eats shit." And the whole
place of drunken sixteen
and seventeen year olds
starts pumping like it's a western.
Tables flying. Bottles breaking.
The sounds of fists and fear.
Then the lights go out/the real thing.
When I got to the door
I saw some Stamfords kicking some guy
from Norwalk as he tried to crawl
up the stairs. And someone from the band
is walking by, almost crying, yelling
"Where's my saxophone?
Who's got my saxophone?" And I look
around and there's Danny Kinaly
hiding behind a table, grinning
like he found a lot of money.
He didn't even need the saxophone.

STEPHEN DUNN

At the Smithville Methodist Church

It was supposed to be Arts & Crafts for a week,
but when she came home
with the "Jesus Saves" button, we knew what art
was up, what ancient craft.

She liked her little friends. She liked the songs
they sang when they weren't
twisting and folding paper into dolls.
What could be so bad?

Jesus had been a good man, and putting faith
in good men was what
we had to do to stay this side of cynicism,
that other sadness.

O.K., we said. One week. But when she came home
singing "Jesus loves me,
the Bible tells me so," it was time to talk.
Could we say Jesus

doesn't love you? Could I tell her the Bible
is a great book certain people use
to make you feel bad? We sent her back
without a word.

It had been so long since we believed, so long
since we needed Jesus
as our nemesis and friend, that we thought he was
sufficiently dead,

that our children would think of him like Lincoln
or Thomas Jefferson.
Soon it became clear to us: you can't teach disbelief
to a child,

only wonderful stories, and we hadn't a story
nearly as good.
On parents' night there were the Arts & Crafts
all spread out

like appetizers. Then we took our seats
in the church
and the children sang a song about the Ark,
and Hallelujah

and one in which they had to jump up and down
for Jesus.
I can't remember ever feeling so uncertain
about what's comic, what's serious.

Evolution is magical but devoid of heroes.
You can't say to your child
"Evolution loves you." The story stinks
of extinction and nothing

exciting happens for centuries. I didn't have
a wonderful story for my child
and she was beaming. All the way home in the car
she sang the songs,

occasionally standing up for Jesus.
There was nothing to do
but drive, ride it out, sing along
in silence.

Walking the Marshland

Brigantine Wildlife Refuge, 1987

It was no place for the faithless,
   so I felt a little odd
walking the marshland with my daughters,

Canada geese all around and the blue
   herons just standing there,
safe, and the abundance of swans.

The girls liked saying the words,
   gosling,
egret, whooping crane, and they liked

when I agreed. The casinos were a few miles
   to the east.
I liked saying craps and croupier

and sometimes I wanted to be lost
   in those bright
windowless ruins. It was early April,

the gnats and black flies
   weren't out yet.
The mosquitoes hadn't risen

from their stagnant pools to trouble
   paradise and to give us
the great right to complain.

I loved these girls. The world
   beyond Brigantine
awaited their beauty and beauty

is what others want to own.
    I'd keep that
to myself. The obvious

was so sufficient just then.
    Sandpiper. Red-wing
blackbird. "Yes," I said.

But already we were near the end.
    Praise refuge,
I thought. Praise whatever you can.

MARTIN ESPADA

Trumpets from the Islands of Their Eviction

At the bar two blocks away,
immigrants with Spanish mouths
hear trumpets
from the islands of their eviction.
The music swarms into the barrio
of a refugee's imagination,
along with predatory squad cars
and bullying handcuffs.

Their eviction:
like Mrs. Alfaro, evicted
when she trapped ten mice,
sealed them in plastic sandwich bags
and gifted them to the landlord;
like Daniel, the boy stockaded

in the back of retarded classrooms
for having no English
to comfort third-grade teachers;
like my father thirty-five years ago,
brown skin darker than the Air Force uniform
that could not save him, seven days county-jailed
for refusing the back of a Mississippi bus;
like the nameless Florida jíbaro
the grocery stores would not feed
in spite of the dollars he showed,
who returned with a machete,
collected cans from shelves
and forced the money
into the clerk's reluctant staring hand.

We are the ones identified by case number,
summons in the wrong language,
judgment without stay of execution.
Mrs. Alfaro has thirty days
to bundle the confusion of five children
down claustrophobic stairs
and away from the apartment.

And at the bar two blocks away,
immigrants with Spanish mouths
hear trumpets
from the islands of their eviction.
The sound scares away devils
like tropical fish
darting between the corals.

HARRY HUMES

My Mother at Evening

This evening with the breeze
blowing the curtains from the window,
my mother tells me again
the story of her young husband
when they lived in the Ash Alley house,
no children, no car, her hair red,
and him with his first mining job
at Packer Number Five, ten miles from home,
how at the end of his shift
he'd come up from the pit in the gunboat,
face black, lips and tongue pink as her peonies,
and not stopping at the washroom,
walk down to the railroad tracks
and wait for a train to hop.

Lunch bucket and tin water bottle
rattling on ropes around his neck,
he'd run alongside when one came through
and, reaching up over the steel wheels
for the ladder, haul himself up
the side of the car and hang there
for the ride back, hoping the train
would not gather too much speed
on the Ashland grade.
Sometimes it did, she tells me again,
and then he'd go right on through.

Not married a year, her eyes then clear,
hair shining, and a blue bandanna rolled
and tied around her head. She'd sit by the crossing,
watching for the engine's powerful lamp

to make everything blaze as it passed,
for him to swing down, smiling,
out of the dark.

I think of them then, walking down the path
into the evening, a few bats over the town,
some children playing hoop-the-lalla
beneath a street light, and my mother
and her husband passing by, almost touching.

MANUEL IGREJAS

Herois do Mar

The sunny, friendly fishermen
of brochure Portugal never made it
to Newark where sober squirrels
filled factories and ditches, carried
money in paper bags to buy homes
jammed Penn Savings Monday nights
with passbooks over their hearts.
Squirrelly instinct in the dark eyes
that lined the altar, of a people
just barely domesticated
awaiting the free meal of communion.
Sunday too was bloody soccer games
with all sides passionately wrong
and wine to solve everything
or make it worse. Wine-stained white shirts
at Sport Club picnics. Accordions and mandolins
in the pavilion. Stately Paso Dobles
and riotous polkas until someone falls

and breaks a leg. Wine in bowls,
chouriço on a spit, purple bread crumbs
on chins. Then it's sweaty busloads home.
A man slaps his wife. Children fall asleep.
A childish people, unread, all passion
and secrets in love, singers in a language
that is its own song
and somehow brave to make in Newark
a scrubbed ghetto of color and comfort
where figs grow fat in tiny gardens
and sardines sizzle all summer long.

X. J. KENNEDY

On the Proposed Seizure of Twelve Graves in a Colonial Cemetery

Word rustles round the burying-ground
Down path and pineconed byway.
The Commonwealth craves twelve heroes' graves
For a turn-lane in its highway.

Town meeting night, debate is slight:
Defenders of tradition
Twitter and cheep, too few to keep
The dead from fresh perdition.

With white-hot gaze emitting rays
Observes Selectman Earnwright,
"Some stupid corpse just wastes and warps
Where traffic needs to turn right!"

Embattled still within his hill,
One farmer loosed a snicker.

"When once ten redcoats dogged my arse,
I did not light out quicker

"Than when in a foss our scraps they'll toss
Therein to blend and nuzzle
Till God's last trump lift skull and rump,
One risen Chinese puzzle!

"Late yesterday as I listening lay
And the sweet rain kindly seeping,
I would have sworn I heard Gabe's horn—
'Twas but rush-hour's beeping.

"Ah, on my life, old Marth my wife
Will soon regret I chose her
When through our bosom-bones protrude
Posterity's bulldozer."

Rose a voice in wrath from under the path:
"Why skulk we in this cavern?
Come, lads, to arms!—as once we formed
One morn at good Fitch Tavern!

"Are we mild milksops nowadays?
Do not we still resemble
The men we were, for all Time's wear?
Repair your bones! Assemble!"

But the first wraith gave a scornful laugh.
"With muskets long outmoded?
We'd stuff the crows like thrown-down grain
Ere our poor barrels we'd loaded.

"For we dead," mused Seth, "but squander breath
On current ears. 'Tis plain
They'd amputate Christ's outstretched arms
To make a right-turn lane."

At the Last Rites for Two Hotrodders

Sheeted in steel, embedded face to face,
They idle now in feelingless embrace,
The only ones at last who had the nerve
To meet head-on, not chicken out and swerve.

Inseparable, in one closed car they roll
Down the stoned aisle and on out to a hole,
Wheeled by the losers: six of fledgling beard,
Black-jacketed and glum, who also steered
Toward absolute success with total pride,
But, inches from it, felt, and turned aside.

GALWAY KINNELL

from *The Auction*

My wife lies in another dream.
The quilt covers her like a hill
of neat farms, or map of the township
that is in heaven, each field and pasture
its own color and sufficiency,
every farm signed in thread
by a bee-angel of those afternoons,
the tracks of her inner wandering.
In this bed spooled out of rock maple plucked
from the slopes above the farm, saints
have lain side by side, grinding their
teeth square through the winter nights,
or tangled together, the swollen
flesh finding among the gigantic

sleep-rags the wet vestibule, jetting
milky spurts into the vessel
as secret as that amethyst glass
glimpsed once overlaid with dust
in the corner of an attic.

MAXINE KUMIN

The Long Approach

In the eel-thin belly of the Metro Swearingen
banking in late afternoon over Boston Harbor,
the islands eleven lily pads, my life loose as a frog's,
I try to decipher the meaning of hope rising up again
making music in me all the way from Scranton
where the slag heaps stand like sentries shot dead
at their posts. Hope rising up in my Saab hatchback,
one hundred thousand honest miles on it as I speed
due north from LaBell's cut-rate autopark
to my spiny hillside farm in New Hampshire.

March 21st. Snow still frosts the manure heap
and flurries lace the horses' ample rumps
but in here it's Stephen Foster coming back to me
unexpurgated, guileless, all by heart.
'Tis summer, the darkies are gay, we sang in Miss Dupree's
fifth grade in a suburb that I fled long ago.
Gone are my friends from the cotton fields away
to—an allusion that escaped me—a better land I know.
O the melancholia as I too longed to depart.
Now I belt out Massa's in de cold cold ground
and all the darkies are a'weepin on route I-93
but what I think of are the french-pastel mornings

daylit at five in my own hills in June when I may
leap up naked, happy, with no more premonition
than the mother of the Pope had. How the same
old pump of joy restarts for me, going home!

What I understand from travel is how luck
hangs in the lefthand lane fifteen miles
over the limit and no cop, no drunk, no ice slick.
Only the lightweight ghosts of racist lyrics
soaring from my throat in common time.
Last week leaving Orlando in a steep climb
my seatmate told me flying horses must be loaded
facing the tail of the plane so they may brace
themselves at takeoff. Otherwise you run
the risk they'll panic, pitch over backwards,
smash their hocks. Landing, said the groom,
there is little we can do for them except
pray for calm winds and ask the pilot
to make a long approach.

O brace me, my groom. Pray for calm winds.
Carry me back safely where the snow stands deep in March.
I'm going home the old way with a light hand on the reins
making the long approach.

Encounter in August

> Black bears are not particularly interested in flesh . . .
> they have been seen in the fields eating string beans.
>
> John McPhee

Inside the teepee that admits
sunlight to the underpart
he stands eating my Kentucky Wonders.
Downs pod after pod, spilling the beans,

the ones I'd saved for shelling out
this winter, thinking *soup*
when he'd gone deep, denned up.

This is not Eden, which ran
unfenced and was not intercropped,
Eden, where frost never overtook a patch.
We stand ten yards apart, two omnivores
not much interested in flesh.
I think he ought to smell me through his greed
or hear my heart outbeat his steady chomp

but nothing interrupts his lunch.
At last he goes the way the skunk
does, supreme egoist, ambling
into the woodlot on all fours
leaving my trellis flat and beanless
and yet I find the trade-off fair:
beans and more beans for this hour of bear.

LYN LIFSHIN

Vacations

my mother preferred
the hotels but toward
the end of two weeks
my father dragged
us down to malden
aunt sophie with warts
like little hills
scrimping on my

mother sister and
my chopped liver
while my fathers grew
like a whole room
tit. later she'd
scold us for xmas
trees and not calling
ben papa or pa. if we
could get thru this
and the skinny snob
of a cousin elaine
and too cheerful
eenie and the
scary inner sanctum
coming thru double
doors we tried to
close two floors
above thered be
bags of candy to
suck on for the car
ride back to vermont
butterscotch tootsie
pops and new hats
for the sun baked
rubber dolls on
the backseat window

Love Canal

Two Poems

chemicals rising
to the surface

poison oozing up to
the surface chemicals
oozing in the back
yard no trespassing
danger signs oily
muck in the street
"if they stay
they're signing
their own death
warrant" on a sign
near a house
candidates come
here days before
the election to
shake hands

its like a ghost
town houses boarded
up I'm afraid if
I leave the house
they'll loot or burn
it I have a child
with birth defects
of heart pancreas
kidney chloroform
was so high it
wouldn't be allowed
in any work place
I was pregnant
the state told me
nothing wasn't
safe

THE NORTHEAST

LEO MAILMAN

Mrs. Greta Freeport Baxter

You imagine that if you were years older
or she years younger, you'd be her Latin
lover and she your Greta Garbo. Realistically,
you'd be the grandson she'd have if she had
ever married. Instead, she lives alone in
the 20-odd room mansion on her acres of property
on the rock-bound coast of Maine. Like a scene

from Dickens or possibly Thomas Hardy, you
sit in the cavernous kitchen and the cook
serves you chocolate cake and milk. All the
people in her life, including you, are hired
to be there. You were hired through Manpower
to tend the gardens as a summer replacement.
You feel at home and feel empathy for the monied
old lady—you tend her lawns and hedges and
flower beds as if they were your own. She asks

what they pay you and doubles the amount. You
row out to her sailing yacht and bask in the
long afternoon sun. You decide that wealth is
a made-to-order garment and fits you well.

The summer's end approaches and her regular
gardener returns from his trip abroad. The old
lady brings you into her home to polish silver.
She wants to retain you forever, but realizes
that you will soon marry and move away to
California. She gives you a hug and a kiss and
a wedding gift in a small white envelope. You

imagine yachting with her to the Caribbean and
tea and cakes served on silver and strolls in
a manicured garden by the sea. You imagine a
youthful Greta who takes your arm in hers.
She guides you to the boathouse on a humid
afternoon where you make torrid love on a pile
of canvas sail. Once you get outside, you tear

open the envelope. Love is a made-to-order
garment and fits you well.

DAN MASTERSON

Bloodline

Her son's back is leather; wet,
it becomes her father's
russet brown, tanned by field weather
however it happened to turn;
it is the Seneca skin he kept hidden in cloth,
like something passed on in shame.

For half her life, she has failed
to bring him back through her son; and again
she kneels at the hill of stones, watching
the boy in the pond below:

He is unaware of the workshirt she sees
come up from the grave
to fit itself to his shoulders,
giving itself to water, as his arms pump
against stalks, cutting a path
toward the opposite shore, long muscles,

almost a man's, pacing themselves,
as the back goes bare, glistening with labor.

He comes up from water, trailing
a branch half his height, and slashes
the weeds as though they were there
waiting to be harvested; her lips move,
unseen, and he is gone,
into the thicket, her hand near, stretched
across the pond, selecting a tree
for its strength.

He climbs a clearing limb, and walks
until it bends, filling his lungs
with sunlight, his shadow
laid like cloth on the pond; he folds
himself in half, and enters without sound,
surfacing a long way from shore,
his gaunt face turning for air,
its features more like her father's
than before.

He will come with grain dripping off him
like water, words tumbling out, a plea
to go with him to see the world he's found;
and she will go,
always she will go, to follow his hands
and something akin to that other voice
giving names to things growing at his feet:
The adder's-tongue and bloodroot, trailing
arbutus, and ahead, bunch berries looking
like fallen dogwoods, lady slippers
near pulpits, Indian pipes white
against the peat moss floor
of an earlier spring
when her father found arrowheads and clover
in the open fields of her hidden life.

GERALD MCCARTHY

Note in a Bottle

The Erie-Lackawanna trains are the ghosts
of summer nights. A town of freightyards,
tanning factories, timeclocks.
A town that smelled like leather.

I walk the ties through yards & loading docks,
remember crawling between rails, watching
the headlights of sheriff cars.

If I listen I can almost hear the sirens,
glimpse the smudge of orange sky beyond
the smokestacks. I push open the door
at Ernie's Grill on the North Side of town,
the Italian side.

His hands stained brown from shoe dye,
John Robinsky cursed the heat, swore
the union would never get in.

It never did. They quit making leather
from cowhide. They closed the factories,
laid-off the workers.

Robinsky raised pigeons because it was
something he could do. We used to watch
them lift off & carry those messages away.

Nobody answered, John. No one heard anything
but that flapping of wings. The gun lifted,
the glass raised. Soot filled years in the attic
with the wire cages; mornings in the steel vats,
the drying sheds. Nobody counted.

A town of mortgages, parking lots.
I turn away, walk home toward my father's house,
toward a light in the window of an upstairs room
that flickers & goes out.

LOUIS McKEE

Salt Peanuts

This afternoon I stood on the corner
of Eighth and Lombard
where Dizzy Gillespie cut his hand
damn near off a man because
he was white and thought
that gave him the right
to harrass any black man who passed
with a look on his face
that might have said I've got money
in my pocket, I'm lucky, and maybe
the look also said something
about not taking any shit from anybody.
Maybe it did. Forty-five years later,
and all the faces that passed me
today were white. Nothing's changed.
Some of the white faces said things
about money, some even about shit,
but none of them seemed worried
about getting harrassed, and none
was likely to have a knife in his pocket
ready to cut into any threat.
No one that passed today looked to me

like they had a trumpet
at home, like they could blow the lights out,
turn the bright day to night
and with quick magician's fingers
steal changes from the quiet sky
and make stars right before my eyes.

WILLIAM MEREDITH

Rhode Island

Here at the seashore they use the clouds over & over
again, like the rented animals in *Aïda*.
In the late morning the land breeze
turns and now the extras are driving
all the white elephants the other way.
What language are the children shouting in?
He is lying on the beach listening.

The sand knocks like glass, stuck by bare heels.
He tries to remember snow noise.
Would powder snow ping like that?
But you don't lie with your ear to powder snow.
Why doesn't the girl who takes care
of the children, a Yale girl without flaw,
know the difference between *lay* and *lie*?

He tries to remember snow, his season.
The mind is in charge of things then.
Summer is for animals, the ocean is erotic,
all that openness and swaying.

No matter how often you make love
in August you're always aware of genitalia,
your own and the half-naked others'.
Even with the gracefulest bathers
you're aware of their kinship with porpoises,
mammals disporting themselves in a blue element,
smelling slightly of fish. Porpoise Hazard
watches himself awhile, like a blue movie.

In the other hemisphere now people
are standing up, at work at their easels.
There they think about love at night
when they take off their serious clothes
and go to bed sandlessly, under blankets.

Today the children, his own among them,
are apparently shouting fluently in Portuguese,
using the colonial dialect of Brazil.
It is just as well, they have all been changed
into small shrill marginal animals,
he would not want to understand them again
until after Labor Day. He just lays there.

PETER MORRIS

The White Sand

The white sand in the ashtray
by the elevator
comes from a beach
but who'd believe it—

there's no sand like this
on any beach near New York City
it's almost twinkling now
in the corporate sunshine
holding its cache of Carefree
sugarless gum wrappers,
burnt Borkum Riff shards
and odd things that look
like spitballs
yes, definitely spitballs
but who'd be throwing spitballs
in a building full of
municipal bond specialists—
and lollipop sticks
you have to ask yourself
who'd be eating lollipops
among Northwestern Mutual Life's
international division (a dress code
of Slenderalls, gray silk blouses)
and those people who stub out
their long, low-tar cigarettes
after one disappointing puff
why do they even bother lighting up
you have to wonder
and above all how
does the sand in the ashtray
stay so white
with only these waves
of human conflict and anxiety
crashing across its shores?

ED OCHESTER

Leechburg, PA

One could almost be happy here.
The corner drugstore, Steinberg's,
like the fifties in Brooklyn
with a window full of surgical
appliances and pantyhose,
and in front on Friday night
a group of hoods
talking about getting laid maybe
but obviously not doing it,
their big dumb dicks
wrapped away like tubular chimes
on the symphony off-night,
like exclamation points
looking for something to happen
on Friday night, at Steinberg's
in Leechburg, Pennsylvania.

ALICIA OSTRIKER

The Pure Products of America

In the middle of the Southeast Asian war
When my poetry students would drive
Down from New Brunswick
To meet in my apartment,

See my family, sit on floor, drink wine—
This one sometimes might
Appear, dressed in his
Bob Dylan outfit, black
Scuffy boots, bluejeans, torn
Flannel shirt, black
Leather motorcycle jacket
And a black hat with a brim
To hide his timid face under.
He didn't talk. Late
In the evening he might extract
From his jeans pocket a many-folded
Piece of paper, and
Read the poem on it, a carnival
Or a barnyard, blowing us
Away. He wasn't actually
In the class, but nobody cared about
Things like that then, and Luke was good in ways
We liked, he despised the war, demanded sex
And love for all, in America's own
Vulgarly exhilarating speech
That cats and dogs can figure out,
Tamping it down with dynamite imagery,
Like Rimbaud, and with cadences
Out of rhythm and blues. We all knew
Boys like that. What happened
To this one, he went west
And somehow wrong, America the Beautiful
Too ugly or too toxic. Underwent
Some jail, some hospital, the medication,
The things the experts did then, when a person
Without a lot of money slid
Into the funny Asian jungle
That's right at home, to ensure
They would never return
With information for us. Luke still writes

159

Me letters, it's about twenty years,
Pages half legible in a childish hand.
He thinks he's a detective, only
They put poison in my head
Is what he says, *It*
Slows me down, baby, the therapy—
I used to write him back
But I wish he'd quit.

RON PADGETT

Sonnet

Lights in daytime indoors make outside
less real until night
falls. Night is falling now, 6
P.M., March 26, 1972, Vermont, USA:
too late for tea and too early for dinner,
reminiscent of the Windsor Diner
on US 5 today: shining silver with red
trim perched over an abyss. Risk
your life for a hamburger? With
mayonnaise and tomato? Outside now
the snow is blue with purple rips,
brown snags, tufts of gray and green
twigs reaching toward treehood. Pretty
soon dark, dinner, smoke & lights out.

DAN SICOLI

dennis

out that door
back in the old
italian neighborhood
we were young boys with sticky hands
anxious to interrogate
the summer night

after supper we'd hurry
to the curb
sucking lemon ice
and wait for the street lights
to flicker
until finally they ignited
all in a row up and down the block
it was magic

as our necks tired
we would lay on our backs
in the street
fascinated as sandflies
and mosquitoes slowly collected
into a swarm of frantic dancers
about our magic lamp

occasionally a car would jerk
to a halt stopping just
a few feet from our bodies
we'd smile
never sensing the danger
as they'd drive slowly around us
honking and waving their arms

once a guy got out
and chased us
he caught you in the alley
and gave you a kick in the pants
i heard his cursing
as i ran up the back steps

in that door
safe and innocent
scratching an arm full of bites
laying low by the curtains
like a submarine below the surface
waiting for the coast to clear

REED WHITTEMORE

The Destruction of Washington

When Washington has been destroyed,
And the pollutants have been silting up for an age,
Then the old town will attract the world's Schliemanns.
What, they will say, a dig! as they uncover
The L'Enfant plan in the saxifrage.

So many plaques, so many figures in marble
With large shoulders and lawman lips
Will have to be pieced together and moved to the new
Smithsonian
That the mere logistics will delight vips.

For how can one pass by a muchness? There will be fund
    drives
With uplifting glosses.
Teams of researchers will mass with massive machinery
At the Rayburn ruin
To outscoop Athens and Knossos.

Dusty scholars will stumble in, looking nearsightedly
At gray façades
Of pillar and portal,
And at curious acres of asphalt,
For clues to the mystery of that culture's gods.

Money of course they will miss,
Since money is spoke not at all on the plaques there,
Nor will they shovel up evidence
That the occupants of the chambers and cloakrooms
Were strangers in town, protecting their deities elsewhere;

But sanctums they surely will guess at,
Where the real and true pieties were once expressed.
If the Greeks had their Eleusinians,
Surely this tribe on the Potomac had mysteries too?
—Having to do, perhaps, with the "Wild West"?

Like most of us sitting here now beside the Potomac,
They will find the Potomac primitives hard to assess.
Oh, may their ignorance be, than ours,
At least less!

RICHARD WILBUR

Transit

A woman I have never seen before
Steps from the darkness of her town-house door
At just that crux of time when she is made
So beautiful that she or time must fade.

What use to claim that as she tugs her gloves
A phantom heraldry of all the loves
Blares from the lintel? That the staggered sun
Forgets, in his confusion, how to run?

Still, nothing changes as her perfect feet
Click down the walk that issues in the street,
Leaving the stations of her body there
As a whip maps the countries of the air.

Shad-Time

Though between sullen hills,
Flat intervales, harsh-bristled bank and bank,
The widening river-surface fills
With sky-depth cold and blank,

The shadblow's white racemes
Burst here or there at random, scaled with red,
As when the spitting fuse of dreams
Lights in a vacant head,

Or as the Thracian strings,
Descending past the bedrock's muted staves,
    Picked out the signatures of things
        Even in death's own caves.

    Shadblow; in farthest air
Toss three unsettled birds; where naked ledge
    Buckles the surge is a green glare
        Of moss at the water's edge;

    And in this eddy here
A russet disc of maple-pollen spins.
    With such brave poverties the year
        Unstoppably begins.

    It is a day to guess
What wide-deploying motives of delight
    Concert great fields of emptiness
        Beneath the mesh of sight,

    So that this boulder, this
Scored obstacle atilt in whittling spray,
    This swarm of shadows, this abyss
        In which pure numbers play,

    Though cloudily astrew
As rivers soon shall be with scattered roe,
    Instant by instant chooses to
        Affirm itself and flow.

PAUL ZIMMER

The Eisenhower Years

Flunked out and laid-off,
Zimmer works for his father
At Zimmer's Shoes for Women.
The feet of old women awaken
From dreams, they groan and rub
Their hacked-up corns together.
At last they stand and walk in agony
Downtown to Zimmer's fitting stool
Where he talks to the feet,
Reassures and fits them with
Blissful ties in medium heels.

Home from work he checks the mail
For greetings from his draft board.
After supper he listens to Brubeck,
Lays out with a tumbler of Thunderbird,
Cigarettes and *From Here to Eternity*.

That evening he goes out to the bars,
Drinks three pitchers of Stroh's,
Ends up in the wee hours leaning
On a lamp post, his tie loosened,
Fedora pushed back on his head,
A Chesterfield stuck to his lips.

The Great Bird of Love

I want to become a great night bird
Called The Zimmer, grow intricate gears
And tendons, brace my wings on updrafts,
Roll them down with a motion
That lifts me slowly into the stars
To fly above the troubles of the land.
When I soar the moon will shine past
My shoulder and slide through
Streams like a luminous fish.
I want my cry to be huge and melancholy,
The undefiled movement of my wings
To fold and unfold on rising gloom.

People will see my silhouette from
Their windows and be comforted,
Knowing that, though oppressed,
They are cherished and watched over,
Can turn to kiss their children,
Tuck them into their beds and say:
    Sleep tight.
    No harm tonight,
    In starry skies
    The Zimmer flies.

THE
SOUTH

GERALD BARRAX

Spirituals, Gospels

Nothing on earth can make me believe them.
I cringe before the weary forgiving
of that lord whose blood whose blood drowned our gods,
who survived the slave pens
where, thrown in by the masters
as bait to control the chattle,
they nevertheless took him, made him blacker
almost than the masters could endure.
Yet still today, still they sing
to be washed white in his glory, sing
of a bitter earth where my confusions deceive me
   with sweet seasons at my door,
   with dream or memory of savanna and plain
      where the lord is elephant and lion;
      jungle where the deaths of lesser gods
         feed back into its own resurrection;
      canopied rainforest, all that life in the trees
at this earth's heaven.
And whales sing in our oceans.

Yet my own blood weakens, freezes
at their sound, the "unearthly harmonies"
alone probing the faith in my doubt,
making me fear the joy that for the duration of the music
crushes resistence utterly, utterly.
And I know that's who I am, what I am
when the souls of Black folk sing.
While the Soul of Black folk sings.

171

JOHN BENSKO

The Wild Horses of Assateague Island

Although the sign says
Do not feed the horses,

my husband cannot help but admire
their docile looks, the delicate size

of their bodies, and the ease
with which they nibble

the crackers from his hands.
He says: *Why waste stale crackers*

when the least we can do
is make friends?

They lean across the picnic table
and stretch their lips.

Losing its fear, a small herd
drifts across the road toward us.

From behind the dunes
a string of ten or twelve

breaks into a run.
The car, he says, *run for it!*

The home movie later shows
tongues licking the windows,

lips and teeth caressing
the hood. My husband's mouth opens.

He is saying: *Sign? What sign?*
Under the perspective

of wild brown eyes peering in.

DAVID BERGMAN

Urban Renewal, Baltimore

Nothing is lost more completely than
the commonplaces of another
age. Sifting the phosphorescent loam,
archaeologists search the site where
Baltimore's first custom house once stood
for fragments which in this damp climate
resist the dark urge to decompose.

And years ago, not far away, I
saved the black Carrara glass façade
of the Anchor Bar & Restaurant,
the waterfront saloon where sailors
fought with the whores who lived upstairs
until the balls of the wrecking crew
laid everything flat for the highway.

One night Bob and Tom and I went out,
and we pried the slick sheets off the wall.
We placed the heavy panels, acid
etched with Deco letters, in a van,

173

then padded the sides to keep the panes
from shattering. By dawn Tom's mother
had her bare attic crammed to the eaves.

Later came accusations and lies,
the falling out of friends, the falling
in of prospects. I'm told our salvaged
front has disappeared from its hideout,
and next that Tom has died of causes
unexplained in another city,
his folks beyond our consolation.

Whatever we loosen from the past,
burns in the solvent of memory.
Stalled at the choked throat of the harbor,
I wait in rush hour traffic, wait
where the Anchor Bar & Restaurant
had been, where tourists now browse boutiques
and the gulls wipe clean the glass-smooth sky.

SALLIE BINGHAM

Two Girls

Perhaps we would never have known what to say to each
    other
had we met when we haunted the Kentucky woods
    together,
you crossing from the house your grandmother cleaned,
I crossing from the house my grandmother owned,
neither of us meeting.

We know the rank smell of the green walnuts,
tender enough to split with a thumb nail,
we know the stain which cannot be washed away.

We saw the wrinkled hide of the shagbark hickory
sag like the skin under our grandmothers' chins,
grandmothers we loved, who taught us hard lessons.

Show me that house, you asked your grandmother,
and she promised to take you, one day.
You liked the tall feather duster
she held high over her head
as stately she moved among the great rooms.

At your house the dusting was done with diapers.

You wanted her feathered scepter for yourself,
and wondered why she laughed at you when you asked.
You were tall as she was, stately as she was,
and with a need for a scepter.

On the other side of the woods my grandmother cro-
     cheted
lace like frost for my first party dresses,
and told me men take your magic, take every drop—
I did not know I had it but I did not want it taken;
yet I longed to whirl in her laces.

Later I crept away from the terror of her stories—
true every one of them—and broke a path
through the honeysuckle jungle in the deep valley
which you were threading from the other side.

We did not meet on the bridge over the creek,
we did not meet in the abandoned cabin
which smelled of men and dogs and whiskey,

we did not meet on the trail beneath the cliff
where the Bloodroot springs and the Jack-in-the-Pulpit
lifts his fearsome hood.

But in our grandmothers' fears we found ourselves
caught and crystalized, darling girls, woods lovers,
who would come in the end to the same patch of trees.

DAVID BOTTOMS

Face Jugs: Homage to Lanier Meaders

From the tailgate of a pickup on the shoulder of Georgia
   52,
from the crafts tent at the White County Fair,
the right face may find you,

or from the wall of the mountain store at Tallulah Gorge,
one face shelved among his many brothers,
the pig-face, the devil-face, the moon-face, may turn
just the right way in the light
in the leaves, in the light tinted by gingham, by walls
of doll clothes and pastel quilts, may turn
to you, his eyes stunned awake by the knowledge
that yours is the face he was meant for.

There is nothing to do then but lift him from the shelf,
nothing to do but hold him
by the window where the light from the wavy pane
makes a mirror of his glaze, your eyes
swimming in his gouged sockets, your cleft on his chin,
your lips floating over his tongue.

You hear again what that tongue is fired to say, the old
admonishment, the clay and the flesh.
But he is simply you, and as you walk to the car,
happy as a man who's found his puzzle's missing piece,
it frightens you to think you might have left him.

And when you get home to the city,
when you move the crystal cherub into the dining room
and place the fern on the mantle, when you
polish the end table and ease him down on slick
    mahogany,
all you feel is gratitude. And you relax on the sofa,
smiling at the melon head, the pancake cheeks,
the yellow, rock-toothed mouth grinning back in deep
    relief.

The Window

On Allgood Road two miles off Georgia 41, you round a
    curve
canopied by pine
and the house leaps out of the trees to meet you.

Upstairs in the far right window she waited for us,
she rocked in the shadows
of the wide magnolia. After school, newly licensed
by the state, we came to her in pairs, in carloads
leaning into that curve, reckless
on spirits, our hearts thrown to her
by the physics of desire,
and swore, no matter what speed we tore from the wheels
of our fathers, we'd seen her

in the upstairs window, a blossom of magnolia
in her hair.
             These affairs got quickly out of hand,
other boys from other schools following suit,
and soon signs were posted,
the shade pulled down on that room for good.
But we came anyway, at night, in caravans
to see her silhouette in the window, evidence enough.

How long did this go on? All spring and summer,
until one boy threw caution too far into that curve.
After that they sealed the window with mortar and brick,
the room itself the shadow of a crypt.

That was half my life ago, and I've not swerved since
into the wrong lane of any curve. Nor forgotten
that house, the thick wreath
of magnolia branches, the zodiac
of white blossoms surrounding the window, the presence
waiting in that room, patient and promiscuous.

TURNER CASSITY

Appalachia in Cincinnati

We who have bridged the river
Find our bridgehead comfortless:
A few square blocks forever;
Limits steel guitars express.

Beyond the surplus stores,
The pawnshops and the storefront missions,

Outer inner-cores,
Blacks pursue their own persuasions.

We, the heart of darkness,
From our beer-and-sawdust floors,
Look past the pavement slickness
Toward the rainy, sooty airs

Of lighted hills above.
You ever comfortable, your houses
Cantilevered wave
On wave above our poor successes,

Pull your drapes more tightly
Or descend from where you view,
Voyeurs, and do your slumming rightly.
Buy us breakfast. How

Exotic, here where necks
Are red and waitresses are minors,
Flannel lumberjackets,
Soulless food in all-night diners.

Occupied Ohio,
World that ends at Clifton Ridge,
World without end or I.O.
U. calls us from Suspension Bridge.

Watch with us one hour.
The second coffees cool, and, lucky,
We see wet skies clear.
Your sun comes to you from Kentucky.

FRED CHAPPELL

Abandoned Schoolhouse on Long Branch

The final scholar scrawls his long
Black name in aisle dust, licks the air
With his tendril double tongue,
Coils up in shadow of a busted chair

And dozes like the farmer boys
Who never got straight the capital
Of Idaho, found out the joys
Of long division, or learned what all

Those books were all about. Most panes
Are gone now and the web-milky windows
Are open to the world. Gold dust-grains
Swirl up, and show which way the wind blows.

K. B. + R. J., cut deep
In a darkened heart on the cloakroom wall.
Now Katherine Johnson and Roger sleep
Quite past the summons of the morning bell.

The teacher sleeps narrow too, on yonder
Side of Sterling Mountain, as stern
With her grave as with a loutish blunder
In the Bible verse she set them to learn.

Sunset washes the blackboard. Bees
Return to the rich attic nest
Where much is stored. Their vocalese
Entrances the native tranquil dust.

TOI DERRICOTTE

Blackbottom

When relatives came from out of town,
we would drive down to Blackbottom,
drive slowly down the congested main streets
   —Beubian and Hastings—
trapped in the mesh of Saturday night.
Freshly escaped, black middle class,
we snickered, and were proud;
the louder the streets, the prouder.
We laughed at the bright clothes of a prostitute,
a man sitting on a curb with a bottle in his hand.
We smelled barbecue cooking in dented washtubs,
   and our mouths watered.
As much as we wanted it we couldn't take the chance.

Rhythm and blues came from the windows, the throaty
   voice of
   a woman lost in the bass, in the drums, in the dirty down
   and out, the grind.
"I love to see a funeral, then I know it ain't mine."
We rolled our windows down so that the waves rolled
   over us
   like blood.
We hoped to pass invisibly, knowing on Monday we would
   return safely to our jobs, the post office and classroom.
We wanted our sufferings to be offered up as tender meat,
and our triumphs to be belted out in raucous song.
We had lost our voice in the suburbs, in Conant Gardens,
   where each brick house delineated a fence of silence;
we had lost the right to sing in the street and damn
   creation.

We returned to wash our hands of them.
to smell them
whose very existence
tore us down to the human.

JAMES DICKEY

Root-light, or the Lawyer's Daughter

That any just to long for
The rest of my life, would come, diving like a lifetime
Explosion in the juices
Of palmettoes flowing
Red in the St. Mary's River as it sets in the east
Georgia from Florida off, makes whatever child
I was lie still, dividing
Swampy states   watching
The lawyer's daughter shocked
With silver   and I wished for all holds
On her like root-light. She came flying
Down from Eugene Talmadge
Bridge, just to long for as I burst with never
Rising never
Having seen her except where she worked
For J. C. Penney in Folkston. Her regular hours
Took fire, and God's burning bush of the morning
Sermon was put on her; I had never seen it where
It has to be. If you asked me how to find the Image
Of Woman to last
All your life, I'd say go lie
Down underwater for nothing
Under a bridge and hold Georgia
And Florida from getting at each other   hold

Like walls of wine. Be eight years old from Folkston ten
From Kingsland twelve miles in the clean palmetto color
                    Just as it blasts
          Down with a body   red and silver buck
          Naked with bubbles on Sunday   root
                    light explodes
          Head-down, and there she is.

CHARLES FORT

The Worker (We Own Two Houses)

My father was a barber-surgeon
for thirty-three years
and a factory worker
for twenty-three of those years.

On Saturdays it seemed as if
the entire Negro section of town
had grown long hair.
The sounds of shears
still vibrate my ears.
I swept clouds into the wastebasket.
The back room contained hard whiskey
bookies and hidden magazines.

When my father came home at seven A.M.
lifting his black aluminum lunch box,
we seven children met him at the door,
knelt, and untied his shoes.
His tired eyes burned lines
into the side of that box.
Each of us wanted left-overs;

we grew older and took turns.
Steel ball-bearings turned in his hands,
given to us as marbles
and the largest on the block.

They made my father a supervisor;
his white friends for eighteen years
now turned from his voice.
Years before the Army
broke his legs in basic training,
fused them for life.

When dust began to fill my father's bones,
I learned how chronic arthritis
can lock together any old man.
From the backroom I heard my name
and a razor being slapped against leather.
With magazines thrown into place
I carried out his clean towels.
I picked up clouds.

GEORGE GARRETT

Long & Short of It:
A Letter to Brendan Galvin

Over Peter Taylor's
brand new wooden fence,
through the green glossy
shine of magnolia leaves,
directly into my back yard,

it could have been the ghost
of Ted Roethke or Big Jim
Dickey in a Halloween costume
or maybe even Galway Kinnell
cultivating that familiar image,
but was in fact a black
bear cub standing about six-four
and coming in at close to
three hundred pounds.
Quick and agile,
he was a real one like
one of yours, Brendan,
good poet of the real and true,
his bristles stiff as a toilet brush
and a strong scent to raise hair
on the neck and back
of my black and tan hound
barking safely in the house.
Bear took one look at me
and the old cop and the young
Ranger with his tranquilizer gun,
then turned and went,
light as Baryshnikov,
over my ragged back hedge,
down the dry creek bed and,
quicker than I ever saw
anything larger than a squirrel
move, vanished into a shimmer
of leaves and afternoon light.
Forever as far as I was concerned.
Cop and Ranger lost him, too,
on the other side of Route 29
in a patch of pine woods near
the football practice field.
And that's about the size,
the long and short of it.

I don't know what it means,
Brendan, except that maybe
even an ordinary backyard
can yield up a share of
surprises. Meantime it gives
me plenty to think about.
I picture the bear, unnoticed,
joining in at football practice,
making the team, going to classes,
and on Saturday playing defense
against Virginia Tech,
first big game we won.
I pictured a Tech player
complaining to his coach:
"Hey, coach, that dude playing
across from me, he's the ugliest
brother I've ever seen.
Got hair all over, head to toe,
red eyes and something like claws,
too; and I'm not going back
out there without a gun."

CHARLES GHIGNA

The Untold Truth about Hank

"Hank never loved nuthin'
like he loved his country music,"
his mother whispered,
looking down at the Bible
she held in her lap.

It was one of those funeral truths
that come out no matter who's listening.
And every silent one of us was,
every one of us already knowing that truth
and a whole bunch more about Hank
we hoped his mother wouldn't whisper.
Like the one about the time he stopped the car,
took it out and relieved himself
right there in the dark along Highway 82,
about how he just left it hanging out
when he got back in behind the wheel,
about how Brenda Sue drew up
from the back seat just to have a look,
about how he showed it to her,
about how she straddled herself
across the front seat,
showing us every layer of crinoline she owned,
about how it looked like some giant, pink,
woman-eating chrysanthemum had swallowed her
all the way up to her waist,
about how she finally settled herself down
in between Bobby and Hank,
about how we watched from the back seat
her bleached blonde head go up and down,
about how Hank kept his eyes on the road
driving faster and faster
until he broke out in a song,
about how he just kept right on singing
long after her head was asleep in his lap,
about how that old Ford made it on down the road
carrying him and his songs and all of us back
to his funeral where we remembered for a moment
this untold truth about Hank.

R. S. GWYNN

A Short History of the New South

"Pass the biscuits," said Pappy, pursing his lips,
But the part I remember best was the collect call
From our spy at the National Archives. "The cause,
I fear, is lost, Suh," the spy replied. "Our retreat
Has been repulsed." "The silver!" cried Mammy
And we grabbed our hoes and headed for Gramma's grave
Expecting the worst. Come spring the worst was over
And we dragged the trunks back up to the big house,
Ending the era with supper and lots of biscuits.
Pappy, picking his tooth, said, "Pass the yams,"
But no one had the heart to tell him the truth.
"Bull Run!" yelled Pee Wee, the subject changed,
And Pappy forgot the yams and got drunk instead.
I woke from my bale of paper money to find
The darkies loading their Cadillacs. They were heading
For Baltimore, they claimed, to harvest the nylon crop.
So we plowed the cotton under and planted magnolias
But missed their singing so much we pawned our whips
To buy a gramophone on the installment plan.
As we had no records, we had to make do without.
"Pass Ol' Blue," said Pappy, closing his eyes,
And nothing improved. Pee Wee got up from the table
And ran off to join the White Sox, where he made
A name for hisself after changing his name. Myself,
I stayed at home to fight the school board. "Hurry back!"
Cried Mammy, waving her flag at the bus.
I took my time. Thursday she called collect:
"Pappy's right poorly. Y'all come." I came,
Arriving in time to grab my hoe from the toolshed
And help Pappy dig her a hole right next to Gramma's.

We cashed the insurance and bought us a TV and rotor,
Which we used to improve our minds and accents,
And when the last of the place was sold off to the tourists
We pooled our cash and built this fine new restaurant.
"Pass the pizza," says Pappy, stroking his silver beard.

HUNT HAWKINS

Mourning the Dying American Female Names

In the Altha diner on the Florida panhandle
a stocky white-haired woman
with a plastic nameplate "Mildred"
gently turns my burger, and I fall into grief.
I remember the long, hot drives to North Carolina
to visit Aunt Alma, who put up quarts of peaches,
and my grandmother Gladys with her pieced quilts.
Many names are almost gone: Gertrude, Myrtle,
Agnes, Bernice, Hortense, Edna, Doris, and Hilda.
They were wide women, cotton-clothed, early-rising.
You have to move your mouth to say their names,
and they meant strength, spear, battle, and victory.
When did women stop being Saxons and Goths?
What frog Fate turned them into Alison, Melissa,
Valerie, Natalie, Adrienne, and Lucinda,
diminished them to Wendy, Cindy, Susy, and Vicky?
I look at these young women
and hope they are headed for the Presidency,
but I fear America has other plans in mind,
that they be no longer at war
but subdued instead in amorphous corporate work,

189

somebody's assistant, something in a bank,
single parent with word processing skills.
They must have been made French
so they could be cheap foreign labor.
Well, all I can say is,
Good luck to you
Kimberly, Darlene, Cheryl, Heather, and Amy.
Good luck April, Melanie, Becky, and Kelly.
I hope it goes well for you.
But for a moment let us mourn.
Now is the time to say goodbye
to Florence, Muriel, Ethel, and Thelma.
Goodbye Minnie, Ada, Bertha, and Edith.

MICHAEL HEFFERNAN

Living Room

Christmas Eve at Beitzinger's Hardware
John & Phil had bourbon in the backroom for the
   customers
along with a cooker full of braised raccoon.

I would have eaten some, only Bill Allen,
who was in there replumbing his toilet,
said This coon is a little blue,

and John had referred to cooking it long enough
to get the strangeness out.
So I drank my bourbon and stepped into the light

on Broadway and went next door to buy
Kathy a wristwatch from Bud Benelli,
who was delighted to see me buy something for a change.

The great thing is, I thought,
that down here in the real world nobody's gods win
and nobody's demons either.

Which is why Phil had placed that poor beast's forepaw
on a piece of hardcrust bread
and laid it in the scalepan where they weigh the nails

and Uncle Bud had seen fit that she should come
into the living room with that watch on
dancing to something on the radio.

DONALD JUSTICE

A Winter Ode to the Old Men
of Lummus Park, Miami, Florida

Risen from rented rooms, old ghosts
Come back to haunt our parks by day,
They creep up Fifth Street through the crowd.
Unseeing and almost unseen,
Halting before the shops for breath,
Still proud, pretending to admire
The fat hens dressed and hung for flies
There, or perhaps the lone, dead fern
Dressing the window of a small
Hotel. Winter has blown them south—

How many? Twelve in Lummus Park
I count now, shivering where they stand.
A little thicket of thin trees.
And more on benches turning with
The sun, wan heliotropes, all day.

O you who wear against the breast
The torturous flannel undervest
Winter and summer, yet are cold,
Poor cracked thermometers stuck now
At zero everlastingly.
Old men, bent like your walking sticks
As with the pressure of some hand,
Surely we must have thought you strong
To lean on you so hard, so long!

DAVID KIRBY

Catholic Boys

At Sacred Heart, if you said you did it,
the priests shouted aloud
and people twisted in their pews
to see who left the little black booth;

once, at Our Lady of Mercy,
Father Becnel dragged Michael Kadair
into the aisle and told him
never to come back, and we wondered
if Mike had confessed to a new grip
of if Father had caught him at it

then and there. The priests raved on,
drunk with fury; nothing fell off
but our faith. Still, to disobey
is painful. We turned serious and pale
and spoke only among ourselves,
and our mothers wept.

Then Eddie Graham saved our souls:
Go to St. Mary's, he said one day,
the priests there have heard everything.
We went, and it was true. God forgave us,
and we took the sacraments again.

Now I am a grown man and a skeptic.
I have a lovely wife.

More Shrines

No, I don't think we would
be orthodox believers
had Charles Martel not
turned back the Moslems
at Tours in 732, thus
allowing the West to
grow up Christian, Jewish,
and, for the most part,
slightly perplexed about
but mainly oblivious to
such matters as good,
evil, and whether or not
we will go to Paradise
when we die. But even
though my hometown of

Tallahassee contains the
name of Allah, and even
though we have Arabic
words in our language,
such as algebra, which
sounds Arabic and even
looks that way, or did
in the eighth grade,
still, this is America,
and while I cannot see
us adopting the placid
temperaments of the
desert people, so
self-composed in their
long, loose robes yet
struggling continuously
with the malicious *djinn*
who rule the kingdom of
death that begins just
a few feet from the oasis,
we need, do we not, more
places in this country
that are solemn and
serene, although there
can be only one holy
stone set in the corner
of the Ka'aba in Mecca,
white when given to Adam
at the time of the fall but
black now from the sins
of those who have kissed it.
I like this: a kind
of sin-magnet that
would pull all of the
wickedness out of us,
because, as it says

in the Koran, you
can run, pretty momma,
but you can't hide.

MARTIN KIRBY

from *Afterlife of a Troll*

Well, I swanee!
If it ain't State Senator Virgil D. Eatbabe,
of Chompsburg, Ark.—
Lovely, trollish target
of my youthful idealistic wrath.
I didn't know you were dead, Virge,
But here you are—
On Plate 457 of the *Audubon Society Field Guide to
North American Fishes, Whales and Dolphins,*
Reincarnated with exquisite verisimilitude
As an Atlantic wolffish—
I'd know that mean-stupid, heavyjawed scowl anywhere.
Here you are, oh, puissant longtime chairman
Of the Joint Committee on Intrastate Pillaging,
Still happily employed at what you always did best—
Squatting on the dark bottom
With your mouth open and your teeth sharp,
Waiting for something small, weak and yummy
To come scooting by.
And I had you figured for just a common garfish, Virge.
Shucks, with karma like yours,
You'll probably just keep sinking right on down.
Hey! You'll love being a Pacific hagfish, Virge,

Like this one on Plate 444.
Just lookit what it says right here on page 324:
"The Pacific hagfish enters the mouth or anus of larger
    fishes and feeds on the insides, leaving only the skin
    and bones."
Whooee! I'd love to be right there, Virge,
Hanging in a shark-proof cage with a movie camera,
When you crawl into the mouth, or gosh! the anus.
Of a Great White Shark.
But, I guess that shark would turn out to be one of your
    late colleagues, Virge,
Doing business as usual.

◆　◆　◆

Well, I guess you won, Virge.
How I longed, twenty years ago,
To see you picking okra at Cummins Prison.
But I see you done died and gone to Heaven.
But, you know, Virge, by the time you bottom out
As an AIDS virus, and can't sink any lower,
All them scientist-folks might have hit on a cure.
What a thought, Virge, to be cured of *you*.
I mean, just think—there you are
In a comfy little lymphatic eddy,
Beatifically digesting the life out of some poor jerk,
And suddenly a gang of strange, tough-looking molecules
Surround you and rip off your protein coat
And stomp you into a pile of ugly little atoms
Which float into the bloodstream, and on inexorably
To the terrible, trash-flushing kidneys.
Wow, Maybe there's design, after all,
And beauty in the design.
But meanwhile, Virge, what a rare pleasure
To close the book on you.

YUSEF KOMUNYAKAA

Landscape for the Disappeared

Lo & behold. Yes, peat bogs
in Louisiana. The dead
stumble home like swamp fog,
our lost uncles & granddaddies
come back to us almost healed.
Knob-fingered & splayfooted,
all the has-been men
& women rise through nighttime
into our slow useless days.

Live oak & cypress
counting these shapes in a dance
human forms aren't made for. Faces
waterlogged into their own
pure expression, unanswerable
questions on their lips.

Dumbstruck premonitions rise
from the heckle-grass
to search us out.
Guilty, sings the screech owl.
I hear the hair keeps growing
in the grave. Here
moss lets down a damp light.

We call back the ones
we've never known, with stories
more ours than theirs.
The wind's low cry
their language, a lunar rainbow

lost among Venus' flytraps
yellowing in frog spittle & downward mire.
Where boatloads of contraband
guns & slotmachines have been dumped
through the years.

Here's this lovely face so black
with marsh salt. Her smile,
a place where minnows swim.
All the full presence
shiny as a skull under the skin.
Say it again—we are
spared nothing.

PAUL LAWSON

Wallis Warfield in Wakefield Manor Days

Visiting through long summertimes, she'd come out
poolside, afternoons, for tea and the japes
of my sister and me. Not everybody liked her,

but we couldn't see why. She was different
from the crowd—talked about Morocco and Spain,
smoked Murads, rode often in a plane.

We gawped when her Ouija board advised
NO SOAP TWENTY-THREE SKIDDOO GO GUAM.
She read our palms, asked what we wanted to be:

My sister cried, "A steeplejack." . . . Me?
What lie could I tell? Venturing "An actor,"
I saw immediately she was pleased.

There was the time I went under in the pool
(the ship was sinking . . . someone was saving me . . .
she kept saying my lips were blue). Dazed,

my teeth chattering, I leaned close beside her,
wrapped in a burnous. (Green fingernails!)
She gave me a sip of her tea. It wasn't tea.

SUSAN LUDVIGSON

Love at Cooter's Carpet, Fort Lawn, S.C.

Daily I go to the carpet warehouse.
The men think I can't make up my mind.
But the truth is, I have fallen in love
with the young ex–football player
who lights the dingy room with his hair.
Even machines can't help him add,
so we spend hours figuring and refiguring
costs—pad and labor, stairs and tax,
his patient golden head bent over the numbers,
the muscles in his arms reflecting shadows
like water under summer clouds.
Each time he starts the motor on the forklift,
slowly pushing that long steel rod
into the center of a roll, then
lifting it out for me to see. Oh—
it's as if an inner sky were opening,
and all his hazy calculations
fall like stars into my heart.

AL MASARIK

Kentucky Woman

men she knew were door to door
all of them wanted to include her
on their rounds

being just past legal age
just recently married she was
flattered by ringing bells

but too shy too scared
to risk answering anything
but her husband's demands

coming home from the tire plant
looking like a coal miner
leaving black marks on the sheets

black marks on her body
laboring till he lost interest
took up hunting & fishing

doused himself with buck lure
stayed away long hours
leaving her recipes & soaps

men smelling of cheap cologne
that mixed with sweat & rubber
& deer piss till she cried out

under the weight of bodies
ringing of bells
Kentucky sky she wore

like a backpack
stuffed with 22 years
of things she did not need.

Boarded Up

sometimes I think we're like
that mint condition '49 Ford
in the garage out back

that beauty the landlady keeps
locked up hidden from neighbors
but visits & admires

rumor says she kept the car
when the tenant-owner died
& he was too blind to drive it

so every 50's boy dream is
gathering cobwebs & dust
still in cherry condition

with nowhere to go
no dangling dice baby shoes
or perfumed skunks

no wet thighs on naugahyde
no back seat forever promises
no do-bop-she-ba

just boarded up & waiting
for an old woman's key quiver
kiss of air & sun & wind.

PETER MEINKE

The Vietnamese Fisherman on Tampa Bay

He stands, feet spread apart, without a pole—
only a line with hook and shrimp he flicks
with an awkward throw like an old slow-pitch
pitcher at a picnic. It goes
maybe twenty, thirty, feet: then, hand
over hand he guides the line toward shore until
with a quick snap of his thin brown wrists
he hooks another whiting, pulls, and lands

it near the sign: KEEP OFF THE GRASS. We think
he can't read English. But he's one hell
of a fisherman—no one else
catches anything worth keeping while sleek
whiting agitate his pail. He can feed
an extended family tonight . . . Last month,
we remember, four Asian boys—all young—
wandered above the Navy Station—NO SWIMMING!

the sign shouts—and one by one marched out,
sinking like toy soldiers, seen by a neighbor
from a house across the street; he raced over
and saved the last, while the mother howled . . .
At lunch, no one says GOOK: we speculate
on war and peace: Do all our Vietnamese
know each other? Are they all lost cousins
in this bleached city far from Tonkin Bay?

Near the fisherman a boy we guess his child
digs with a stick, steady as a mole
burrowing to China. Beside the hole

a fish snaps like a patient gone wild
in electric shock. Compared to microphones
and disks—our world of stocks and portable
computers—the scene looks elemental,
solid, the tattered players more composed

than we, natty in blazers, suits and ties.
Our work seems artificial, chintzy
as plastic pink flamingos. Fishing
and digging, one says, at least are real. I try
to imagine coming home at end of day
with a bucket of fish. Fishing is real,
I'll tell them. Whiting, sea trout, mackerel.
No shit, Ho Chi Minh, my kids will say.

ERIC NELSON

Everywhere Pregnant Women Appear

Riding bicycles up hills,
lapping pools, volleying for serve.
There's one on any park bench, two
in any restaurant, three in any crowd.
In museums they gaze at the Rubens.
They're knee-deep along the beach
and up to here in advice.

Everywhere pregnant women appear
immaculate, shapely as pears.
Breasts like pears, buttocks
like pears, belly the biggest pear.

What they put in their grocery carts!
A whole cow t-boned, burgered, Delmonicoed.
Anything two-for-one, milk enough
to make Zion the land of just honey.

Everywhere pregnant women appear
like balloons rising over a fair.
Everyone watches their big tops billow
fuller than Barnum & Bailey's. Underneath,
the jugglers and tumblers, flying
trapeezers, lion-tamers, clowns,
tight-rope walkers and bare-back riders
limber up for their appearance.

Columbus of the Alphabet

Where everything once was shriek
and pitch, throat-ruddered lurch
or blubbering of the malcontent,

now mouth steers steadily
toward the spices and silks
of the new world, words.

Commander of his high-chair, he
signals with outstretched arm
whatever wonders catch him

by shape or color, motion or sound—
pinwheel, clock face, backfire.
He claims all in the name of Knowing:

Buh: his mother, her breasts, me,
my beard, cat and dog, toys, food,
bib, light, telephone, everything

beyond the round world of himself
which he rolls to any edge and looks
to this other world, flat

as a syllable, where tree and sky
aren't separate but a single
brown, blue and green thing: Buh:

a good word for a world so whole.
Yet even now his eyebrows, recently
realized, wrinkle downward.

A piece of paper like a sail
billows and dies in a fan's wind.
He opens his mouth but there's more

or less to this than he knows,
motion without motive, object without form.
He can't say where this wind has blown him.

PETER SCHMITT

Glance

It happens hundreds of times each year
in the South, those nights before or after
the hottest of the summer. Someone
will be walking in the direction of home
after closing down a bar,
his body heat lifting
like his troubles
so completely and momentarily
from the insurge of alcohol,

that the warmth of the smooth paved road
stretching before him
will reach out like a familiar bed
or lover and take him in its arms
to sleep. She might have been
just accepting that invitation,
there in the middle of the street,
where the trees arched
and formed a tunnel. In the brief
cone of my headlights she was holding
to the ribbon of yellow paint, and in the flash
of our eyes meeting she seemed not frozen
like an animal, but lost, looking
for something. In a second's swerve
I was past her, yet managed to fix her
once in the mirror, till the road curved
and she vanished. And in no version
of her life will I ever come that close—
at best one backward glance, then gone.

DAVE SMITH

The Tire Hangs in the Woods

First it was the secret place where I went to dream, end
of the childhood road, deep-tracked, the dark
behind my best friend's house, blackberry
thickets of darkness, and later
where we stared, with our girls, into the sky.

Past the hedgerow and the house-stolen fields, past
the wing-shooting of crow remembered, I drive
bathed by green dashlight and the sun's
blood glinting on leaves just parted, then see

again the dead-end, the dying woods, that stillness still
ticking like throat rattle—and Jesus Christ
look at the beer cans, the traffic, even
hung on a berry vine somebody's rubber,

and wouldn't you know it that tire still hangs.

◆

In the Churchland Baptist Church the hot ivy hung,
      smelling
of dust, all mouths lifting their black holes
like a tire I kept dreaming. Clenched
by mother and father who stank sweetly in sweat.
I sang and sang until the black ceiling
of our house seemed to bellow with storm
and the tire skulled against my eyes
in time with the great clock in the far hall.

Hanging in darkness, like genitals, it made me listen.

◆

Years pass like Poe's pendulum into memory, where I see
one summer night I came to fistfight Jim Jenrett,
whose house she came to and she no more now
than a frail hand on my cheek, and I
am beer-brave and nearly wild with all
the dozen piling from cars. Jesus,
look at us in the ghost-flare of headlights,

pissing, taunting, boy-shadows all right,
and me in the tire spinning my childish words.

We pass also, and are blind, into the years like trees
that I cannot see into except to imagine Jim,
dunned by our words, as he goes out
near dawn and steps in the tire
and shies up the electric extension cord, noosed,
by the rope whose tire, burdened, ticks slowly.

◆

Ghost-heart of this place, of dreams, I give you a shove
and sure enough I hear the tick and all that was
is, and a girl straightening her skirt walks
smack against you and screams. You know
who laughs, smoking in the dark, don't you?

There are no headlights now, only the arc of blackness
gathering the hung world in its gullet. Blink
and maybe he's there, his great feet jammed
halfway in the hole of your heart,
gone halfway.

◆

Where do they go who once were with us on this dream
    road,
who flung themselves like seed under berry-
black nights, the faces black-clustered,
who could lean down and tell us
what love is and mercy and why now

I imagine a girl, mouth open in the sexual O, her hair
gone dull as soap-scum, the husband grunting
as his fist smacks again, the scream

not out yet, nor the promise
she could never love anyone else.

I climb in the tire, swinging like a secret in the dark
woods surrounded by the homelights of strangers.
She swore she loved me best.

◆

In the church I imagined this place forever behind me
but now I sit here and try to see the road begin.
Blackberries on both sides blackly hang.
Tall trees, in blackness, lean back at me.
When will they come, the headlights washing
over me like revelation, in cars
ticking and swirling?

Once when my mother could not find me, they came
      here.
He said "So this is it, the place." It was dark,
or nearly, and she said I might have died.
I asked them what being dead was like.
Like being blind or flying at night.

I shove my foot at the dirt and swing in absolute black.
The whine of the rope is like a distant scream.
I think, so this is it. Really it.

   for Robert Penn Warren

LEON STOKESBURY

Lauds

Even in Texas there's a rose on the air
for that quick half-hour during summer dawn.
And we, *new meat*, the summer "college boys,"
began our first good look at things
that thirty minutes before time
when the *permanents* came in
to the Texas State Highway Department barn
to sip the liquor of a cup of coffee—
and then go.

Rysinger would not shut up.
No one could shut him up.
Rysinger was our fathers' age,
and every day brought his constant routine,
each morning commencing as a string of jokes
dirtier than the day before. Each day:
if he could gargle forth some image, some
froth,
so strange to the *new meat*
that it could make us turn our eyes—
then that would make him grin and giggle.
Each day.

But now when I think of Rysinger,
I do not think first of that morning
Plaunty came back from his honeymoon
and Rysinger followed him around asking:
Plaunty?
Why is Plaunty's mouth all puckered up?
What you been eating Plaunty

to cause your mouth to pucker so? Lemons?
Lemons, Plaunty?
And neither do I think of Rysinger's story
of getting two milkshakes down at Dick's Drive-In, nor
of his particularly energetic rendition of The Tale
of Grandpa's French Ticklers, which
brought old Grandma back to life, which
made her go "Whoa!" and then
"Oh!" and then
"Soooooieeeee!"

What I always remember about Rysinger
is the two or three time that summer
along about three or four in the afternoon
when the heat on some country road was killing us,
and the hot asphalt would steam up in our faces,
would billow and speckle our clothes and faces,
and there was nothing but heat,
the world being endless waves of heat—
and I would look over and see Rysinger
trying to hide his red eyes,
making gestures that tried to imply
it was the steam, or the wind,
or the sweat in his eyes,
that made them burn,
there,
by the side of the road.

DABNEY STUART

from *The Opposite Field*

3

I had not thought to find
you so bound,
so driven into the wood.

In the sour locker rooms
we both remember—stretching
their dim tunnels from the first
wet practice all the way
to marriage—some dog
would have said, *'Smatter, lost
your balls?*
          and you would have conned
him so casually, with such play—
the whole team watching—
he'd have thought you wanted
to borrow his.
          Instead,
in the thick heat of Houston,
on real grass, under a glazed dome
of sky and no one watching,
you fungo flies to your son,
to me. The thin *tick* of the wood
on the ball rehearses
itself endlessly, routine
grounder, routine pop-up, big
out *tick* routine:
          after an hour
I take the bat, wave you deep
down the green reaches, stroking

them high and long, driving
you to the wall again
and again, up against it time
after time, and then *over*
the wall, Lord, into the next
field,
    farther,
        the next season,
until I don't know where
you are, have never known . . .
              wanting
your will and heart to keep
from breaking—impossible—
your release into the fabulous spaces.

4 A Lyric Meditation on Sour Locker Rooms

Almost always underground, dank,
at least one corner stinking of piss;
pasty men in cages, doling; bodies
being numbered, uniformed, strapped—
dogsbodies, Dog days, even in mild April.
           Can you go up
from this cavern of mock cells, single file,
into the blare of the green field,
virgin again, lined, and can you
remember how to come back down, the place
empty with you in it, alone, benched, cracked
in bone and will, soaked in your own sweat,
the concrete damp under your bare feet, steamed,
and no shower quite able to drown
the echoes of the metal door opening,
closing,
    the crowd stunned by the high arc
of the ball hung in the glare, against the dark.

HENRY TAYLOR

Projectile Point, Circa 2500 B.C.

In the garden in high summer as the sun dropped,
I worked my hoe in short scythe-swings
until one stroke turned a pebble I stopped to pick up.
I stood pinching it, thumbing off earth crumbs;

this has happened before, but not to me.
There were dozens of these in a black japanned box
in my grandfather's bedroom, which was also
his grandfather's bedroom. In the days when men

plowed the fields behind horses, sunup to sundown
watching the furrow open up and lie over,
three paces ahead of their feet, there was time
to reach down midstride and pocket a recognized stone.

At such times a man might fall to imagining,
but why not stick to such facts as may be?
It is broken at tip and base: botched,
chipped at the end of a shaft-flight,

or lost until it broke under the plow;
and such facts as there are now include
one hot afternoon when I stood sole-deep
in soft ground, wondering at the four thousand years

between the two men who had touched this stone,
guessing how it was not to care
for the magic I felt flowing out of it,
but just to stand here, touching only an implement

like a hoe or a pitchfork, watching the ground
as I watched it, not thinking of the sun
moving on as it moved over me, as it will
when the rocks and the water are alone here again.

JAMES WHITEHEAD

His Slightly Longer Story Song

She was older, say, thirty-five or so,
And I was eighteen, maybe. She was dark
And musical, I thought, out of a book
I hadn't read, Louisiana slow,
A chance to get my ass shot off or grow
Up quickly, outdistancing the nervous pack
Of boys I ran with. I was green but trick
By trick she taught where innocence could go
When what I wanted happened. Innocence
Or ignorance? Or neither one? Or both?
She claimed she'd taken sweetness from my life.

She cried, imagining the pretty wife
I'd hammer with some grief. She said the breath
Of love—this kind—was mostly arrogance.
She'd drink and then she'd dance
Alone and naked to the radio.
She said I was her baby. I said no.
She said in time I'd throw
Away her memory. I knew she lied.
I said I loved her body, loved her pride.

MILLER WILLIAMS

Wiedersehen

When open trucks with German prisoners in them
passed in convoy through the small town
I dreamed in, my fourteenth year, of touchable breasts
and cars and the Cards and the Browns, we grabbed the shirts
we twisted and tied for bases and chased the trucks
past all our houses slow as we could run.

We tossed the baseball up to one of the guards
who sometimes pretended to keep it but threw it back.
Once I threw it badly. A German caught it.
A boy barely older than I was and blonder
and nearly as thin. He grinned and I thought how much
the baseball belonging to John Oscar Carpenter
must have cost. The guard didn't seem concerned
about the baseball or me. We ran for blocks
behind the flatbed truck. The side rails rattling
made the same sense the Germans did
calling and tossing the ball to one another.

We ran in silence needing our breath to breathe
and knowing that begging raises the value of things.
At the edge of town the convoy speeded up.
Everyone stopped but me and the truck pulled away.
I looked back once to see the seven others
standing on the curb of the last street
loose and surprised as a group on a picnic
looking into a river where someone has drowned.

When I turned back to the trucks, pumping my arms,
the pain in my side coming to punish me hard,

to burn the blame away and make us even,
even John Oscar Carpenter and I,
the young German hauled back and let the ball
fly in a flat arc from center field.
I caught it. I held it in the hand I waved
as truck by truck the convoy shifted gears.
"Wiedersehen," he yelled. A word I knew.
I turned and pegged the ball to home in time.
I wondered if he had killed the Rogers boy
or thrown the hand grenade at Luther Tackett
that blew his arm away. I had done something
nobody ever had done. It was large and frightful.
We walked in amazement awhile and went to our houses.

Your grandchildren, German, do they believe the story,
the boy in Arkansas, blonder than you?

Thinking about Bill, Dead of AIDS

We did not know the first thing about
how blood surrenders to even the smallest threat
when old allergies turn inside out,

the body rescinding all its normal orders
to all defenders of flesh, betraying the head,
pulling its guards back from all its borders.

Thinking of friends afraid to shake your hand,
we think of your hand shaking, your mouth set,
your eyes drained of any reprimand.

Loving, we kissed you, partly to persuade
both you and us, seeing what eyes had said,
that we were loving and were not afraid.

If we had had more, we would have given more.
As it was we stood next to your bed,
stopping, though, to set our smiles at the door.

Not because we were less sure at the last.
Only because, not knowing anything yet,
we didn't know what look would hurt you least.

CHARLES WRIGHT

Virginia Reel

In Clarke County, the story goes, the family name
Was saved by a single crop of wheat,
The houses and land kept in a clear receipt for the subse-
    quent suicides,
The hard times and non-believers to qualify and disperse:
Woodburn and Cedar Hall, Smithfield, Auburn and
    North Hill:
Names like white moths kicked up from the tall grass,
Spreading across the countryside
From the Shenandoah to Charles Town and the Blue
    Ridge.

And so it happened. But none of us lives here now, in any
    of them,
Though Aunt Roberta is still in town,
Close to the place my great-great-grandfather taught
    Nelly Custis's children once
Answers to Luther. And Cardinal Newman too.
Who cares? Well, I do. It's worth my sighs

To walk here, on the wrong road, tracking a picture back
To its bricks and its point of view.
It's worth my while to be here, crumbling this dirt
    through my bare hands.

I've come back for the first time in twenty years,
Sand in my shoes, my pockets full of the same wind
That brought me before, my flesh
Remiss in the promises it made then, the absolutes it's
    heir to.
This is the road they drove on. And this is the rise
Their blood repaired to, removing its gloves.
And this is the dirt their were made of, the dirt the world
    is,
Immeasurable emptiness of all things.

I stand on the porch of Wickliffe Church,
My kinfolk out back in the bee-stitched vines and weeds,
The night coming on, my flat shirt drawing the light in,
Bright bud on the branch of nothing's tree.
In the new shadows, memory starts to shake out its dark
    cloth.
Everyone settles down, transparent and animate,
Under the oak trees.
Hampton passes the wine around, Jaq toasts to our health.

And when, from the blear and glittering air,
A hand touches my shoulder,
I want to fall to my knees, and keep on falling, here,
Laid down by the articles that bear my names,
The limestone and marble and locust wood.
But that's for another life. Just down the road, at
    Smithfield, the last of the apple blossoms
Fishtails to earth through the shot twilight,
A little vowel for the future, a signal from us to them.

THE
OLD
WEST

MARY CROW

Going Home

The eye of the dead beer can lives in my headlights.
The Elkhorn Motel flashes "Vacancy"—
only a couple of truckers too tired for love
have registered.
Near the top of the hill,
a sign commands,
"Thru Traffic Take the Center Lane,"
and I drive straight thru without slowing down.

The five women I've just left
are driving home in separate cars.
Late at night, after wine,
we have been talking
about how to meet a man,
about what to do with ourselves.
One woman says,
"I'm in love with my right hand,"
and we all laugh.

We park in front of dark houses
and enter to silence
I turn on a light,
grab a cold beer from the fridge,
and sit by myself in front of the TV.
The light registers in my eyes
but my mind is driving toward love.
Maybe I could post a sign
beside the front door,
"Vacancy."
Maybe I could stand beside the road

and hitch a ride with a trucker.
Maybe I could drive up to a full motel
and knock at the first door.
Maybe I could get in the car and keep driving,
driving thru loneliness
to the other side.

STEVE FISHER

Weather Nose

Winter,
at midnight,
in a late August
Arizona mountain wind:

   Encroaching

   Off-season

with nine pages
of calendar weight,
left
till parole.

JON FORREST GLADE

Sex Education

The nor'wester that passed over the valley
dropped a foot of snow.
The wind kicked up
and the heifers started twinning.
I don't remember if it was '56 or '57
or if I was seven or eight.
What I do remember
is that it was bitterly cold
and we were both caked with frozen blood.

My father would reach far back into the womb,
untangle limbs, turn bodies around
and slip chains over hooves.
Calves are pulled with a block and tackle.
If you save one of two twins, that's good.
If you don't lose the mother, that's better.
Sometimes we'd bring a calf into the house,
give it a drink of warm milk and brandy,
bed it down on straw
in the basement or the bath tub.
A calf is money on the hoof;
you can't afford to lose too many.

That morning my father asked if I knew
the facts of life.
I said I didn't know what he meant.
He said he meant fucking, pregnancy,
childbirth and stuff like that.
I said sure, I knew all about that.
He said, "Yeah, I figured you did.
When I tell you, pull the chain taut."

225

The Weight of the Sheets

Almost bought a machete
that I saw in the window
of the surplus store,
but its hilt fit my hand
just a little too well,
and old memories broke through barriers
that were disappointingly thin;
I was back in the jungles
of the Nam, once again.
I felt the oriental sun
on the back of my neck,
as the temperature rose
and I started to sweat.
So I slid the blade
back in its sheath,
and went and had a drink
in the bar across the street.
There are no guns in my house
and no tricks up my sleeve;
I'm all over that now
I claim I believe
but my wife says I curse
and cry and talk in my sleep.
And I know for a fact
that sometimes my scars
cannot bear
the weight of the sheets.

Blood Trail

I had a man in my sights
and I pulled the trigger.
I knew he would fall,
but I didn't think
he would get back up
and run like a wounded deer.
I was amazed and forgot to shoot again.

We followed the blood trail
that found only an abandoned pack.
The Lieutenant took the cash,
the men divided the food,
Intelligence was sent the love letters
and I got the credit
for a probable kill.
Intelligence reported the letters
were from a woman in the southern provinces.
Which meant she was arrested,
beaten, raped, locked in a tiger cage,
forced to eat her own excrement
and beaten again.

If she confessed, she was executed.
If she refused to confess, she was executed.
It was a funny way.
I shot a man.
I killed a woman.

ANSELM HOLLO

In the Land of Art

the artists
work on the art farm.

They store the art they make
in the art barn.

Once in a while, they take some out
& take it to the art store.

When the art store sells some,
they take their share
& put it in the art bank.

Then they take their art check books
& go to the art inn
to have a good time.

Or take each other to an art movie
or an art dance.

They wash their clothes at the art laundromat
unless they are successful & rich & have
their own art washer & dryer
in their art basement.

When the artists take a trip
(an art trip)
they stay at the art hotel

When they get sick, they go to the art hospital.

& when they die, they're buried
in the art cemetery.

& that's the life of the artists
in the land of art.

WALTER McDONALD

The Night of Rattlesnake Chili

Only the lure of a rattler kept us
jerking dry tumbleweeds back
from the bunkhouse. Already, cook had
chili boiling, peppers and beef
convincing us all we were starving.

Cursing, throwing empty bean cans
at our horses, cook swore he'd douse
the fire and dump our dinner to the mules
unless we brought him a long dry tail
of rattler. I had heard of cooks

crazy enough to grind rattles
like chili powder, a secret poison
to make a pot boil darker than whiskey.
Kicking and calling each other names,
we scoured the yard for an hour,

a ranch so cursed with snakes
jackrabbits weren't safe while mating.
At last, I grabbed one by the tail,

the writhing muscle trying to escape
down a burrow, and Billy Ray shot it.

Cook cut off the tail and grinned,
held up the ticking rattle, then
crushed and ground it in his hands.
Hulls floated down into red steam,
and simmered. That night, we ate

thick chili redder than fire
and griped about the dust and hulls,
but begged for seconds. Even our beer
was cold and sweeter than most
and steel spoons melted in our mouths.

NAOMI SHIHAB NYE

The Saddest Cowboy in Texas

Because he is sitting at the bar
watching ice melt in predictable rhythms,
the prairie rolls under the door
and sleeps in his pocket.
Because he does not answer the women
who ask why he is quiet,
he earns the right to be quiet.

Sometimes he is an eclipse,
he looks at you and you are not there.
He learns to blot out what fails him,
to tune his sight to the sky and the tree.

When a wagon train rattles past
he must live with it, the sound of hooves
disappearing into air.
For days something inside him
pushes west, farther than the land
or his own skin can let him go.

Blood

"A true Arab knows how to catch a fly in his hands,"
my father would say. And he'd prove it,
cupping the buzzer instantly
while the host with the swatter stared.

In the spring our palms peeled like snakes.
True Arabs believed watermelon could heal fifty ways.
I changed these to fit the occasion.

Years before, a girl knocked,
wanted to see the Arab.
I said we didn't have one.
After that, my father told me who he was,
"Shihab"—"shooting star"—
a good name, borrowed from the sky.
Once I said, "When we die, we give it back?"
He said that's what a true Arab would say.

Today the headlines clot in my blood.
A little Palestinian dangles a truck on the front page.
Homeless fig, this tragedy with a terrible root
is too big for us. What flag can we wave?
I wave the flag of stone and seed,
table mat stitched in blue.

I call my father, we talk around the news.
It is too much for him,
neither of his two languages can reach it.
I drive into the country to find sheep, cows,
to plead with the air:
Who calls anyone *civilized*?
Where can the crying heart graze?
What does a true Arab do now?

SIMON ORTIZ

Canyon de Chelly

Lie on your back on stone,
the stone carved to fit
the shape of yourself.
Who made it like this,
knowing that I would be along
in a million years and look
at the sky being blue forever?

My son is near me. He sits
and turns on his butt
and crawls over to stones,
picks one up and holds it,
and then puts it into his mouth.
The taste of stone.
What is it but stone,
the earth in your mouth.
You, son, are tasting forever.

We walk to the edge of cliff
and look down into the canyon.
On this side, we cannot see
the bottom cliffedge but looking
further out, we see fields,
sand furrows, cottonwoods.
In winter, they are softly gray.
The cliffs' shadows are distant,
hundreds of feet below;
we cannot see our own shadows.
The wind moves softly into us.
My son laughs with the wind;
he gasps and laughs.

We find gray root, old wood,
so old, with curious twists
in it, curving back into curves,
juniper, piñon, or something
with hard, red berries in spring.
You taste them, and they are sweet
and bitter, the berries a delicacy
for bluejays. The plant rooted
fragilely into a sandy place
by a canyon wall, the sun bathing
shiny, pointed leaves.

My son touches the root carefully,
aware of its ancient quality.
He lays his soft, small fingers on it
and looks at me for information.
I tell him: wood, an old root,
and around it, the earth, ourselves.

GREG PAPE

Storm Pattern

On my livingroom wall hangs a Navajo rug
handwoven by Virginia Yazzie. A Storm Pattern
with a black and white border, through which
the spirit line passes, a design like silhouettes

of mesas on the Colorado Plateau. Within the border
it's red, Ganado red, with black and white
figures, the sacred water bugs, the mountains
and the clouds, and the intersecting lightning bolts

that shoot out from the center to the four corners.
I love to look at it hanging on my wall.
I love to run my fingers over the wool.
Virginia Yazzie also raised and tended the sheep

and sheared the wool and spun it by hand,
mixing in a little hair from her goats.
She dyed the wool and she built the loom
on which to weave it. She made up

this variation on the old pattern, and
she took pleasure in the work of her hands.
But there's coal and uranium and maybe oil
on her land, and the government says she

and her family have to move, relocate
is the word they use, to Flagstaff or Winslow
or Tuba City. Think of Virginia Yazzie
with the relocation blues. Imagine her

telling the government she'll never move.
Then remember the water bugs, the mountains,
the clouds, the lightning, the border through which
the spirit line passes, the storm pattern in her eyes.

ALBERTO RIOS

Incident at Imuris

Mr. Aplinio Morales has reported this:
They were not after all
Watermelons, it was not the wild
Fruit patch they at first had thought;
In the manner of what moths do,
These were cocoons, as every child has
Picked up and squeezed,
But from in these came and they saw
Thousands of green-winged half moths,
Half moths and not exactly butterflies,
Not exactly puppies—
A name for them did not exist here.
Half this and some of that,
What was familiar and what might be European.
And when the fruit rotted, or seemed to rot—
Almost all of them on the same day—
From out of each husk the beasts flew
Fat, equipped, at ease
So that they were not so much
Hungry as curious.
The watermelons had been generous homes.
These were not begging animals,

Not raccoons, nor rats,
Not second or third class;
These were the kind that if human
They would have worn dinner jackets
And sniffed, not at anything in particular,
Just as general commentary.
Animals who had time for tea.
Easily distracted and obviously educated
In some inexplicable manner,
The beasts of the watermelons left
The same day, after putting their heads
In windows, bored already
From chasing the horses
And drinking too much from the town well.

Singing the Internationale

We heard the stories big-screen like,
Martí did this, Sandino over there,
Jara later without his fingers,
How the *Internationale*'s words were
Meant to be sung.
They were all the never quite in front of us,
The invisible and secret,
Aunts and uncles, José, César,
Victor Jara who was, possibly, my grandfather,
Or his brother, which did not so much matter.
What counted was when he played the mandolin
Once on a train as a musician—
This is what he said he was,
Not a lawyer, which was fact—
And so escaped the Villista's bullet,

But with a rifle held
To his temple as he played.
And the great Doroteo Arango himself,
My wandering great-uncle
On the other side of the family,
Who dropped his coffee once
Staining the rug of my Great-aunt Gabriela,
Her only rug, and so she scolded him,
With force. *Pancho Villa indeed,* she said.
And he had to come back to face the debt.
She made him promise.
Desgraciado, she called him, and pinched
His fat ear in the beak of her two fingers.

KIRK ROBERTSON

drawing to an inside straight

dust swirls behind you
down Indian Lakes road

almost there
you tell yourself

no longer sure why
you're going what
will happen

when you get there
fish and white pelicans

do you remember the time
your son slipped under
gagging spitting
as he broke the surface
glad to see the sky

the time you came
on a picnic

today there's nothing
only what the wind
left behind

muttering
in the trees

yeah, yeah
shut up and deal

driving to Vegas

Tonopah's
the only place
contour lines
appear
to rise

between there
and Goldfield
the first
Joshua trees

beer at the Mozart Club

from then on
it's all downhill

between Mercury
and Indian Springs
the light
begins to change

you wonder
what you'll do
when you reach
the edge
of the map

out there
on the horizon

all that neon

beckoning you

in from the dark

REG SANER

Where I Come From

Where I come from the bright ones
left the farm. What this picnic snap
doesn't show is Uncle Cyril
who wanted to write for the slicks
selling Porta-Pools, the *Americana,* cable TV.

And what Grandad Rexroat can't see here
is how a man could lose
even this land we're standing on.
Uncle Frank's first, Aunt Maude, hates
his farming so much she pours dishwater
into his lap before taking off. Her big idea
is L.A. Aunt Minta writes she's there yet,
visiting Helen Frances up in Palm Springs
while Frank switches wives like two-tone shoes.
Mail from Uncle Lee in Fort Wayne plugs thrift,
the G.O.P., and Kroger stores
because he owns stock. In Omaha
the feed-cattle Grandad buys to come back
can't quite believe in his luck, so he develops
a window-screen/storm-window route,
raking leaves off the rich end of town.
Each birthday card has heft, its 50-cent piece
Scotch-taped, fire-new from the mint.
I answer by pencil, each word fat,
but never answer enough. From Toledo
Uncle Cyril considers retiring early on fiction
he's still planning to write. This picnic's
our last where Grandmother Rexroat
has full use of both hands. RM lolls
in sandals and curls on that wide
hammock of staves. The elms go deep.
The new porch's paint looks fresh
to the touch. I can see that towheaded
dwarf they're aiming into the lens
hasn't a clue how far
he's squinting from there,
with somewhere a city for each of us.

GARY SHORT

Near the Bravo 20 Bombing Range

I bring the mare a green apple, then ride
the wrinkled land along the river road
in the slow-turning wheel of the day.
Past the pen of the brown goat with the broken moan,
past the stiff glove thick with dirt
where it has lain on the path since winter,
past the coyote slung over the barbed fence,

its eyes gone to sky—
blue where a black jet angles
high above the stand of aspen, the leaves
spinning to coin in the wind's hand.
I ride past the green wave of alfalfa
that grows one sweet inch each day.

Over the next mountain is the range,
public land bombed for thirty-five unauthorized years.
At what point is turning back an option?
The skeleton of a mustang, dreaming its run,
rises slowly back out of dust.

Farther out, the surface of the marsh is sunstruck tin.
The ones who walked here before
walked quietly & believed the green
slick on the pond.
I hear the jet after it is gone.
What remains—a white strand, sheer against the sky,
with the breath of the mare
as she bends to drink
from the still water.

GARY SOTO

Mexicans Begin Jogging

At the factory I worked
In the fleck of rubber, under the press
Of an oven yellow with flame,
Until the border patrol opened
Their vans and my boss waved for us to run.
"Over the fence, Soto," he shouted,
And I shouted that I was American.
"No time for lies," he said, and pressed
A dollar in my palm, hurrying me
Through the back door.

Since I was on his time, I ran
And became the wag to a short tail of Mexicans—
Ran past the amazed crowds that lined
The street and blurred like photographs, in rain.
I ran from that industrial road to the soft
Houses where people paled at the turn of an autumn sky.
What could I do but yell *vivas*
To baseball, milkshakes, and those sociologists
Who would clock me
As I jog into the next century
On the power of a great, silly grin.

MAURA STANTON

Returning to Arizona

Martians sent to Earth disguised as humans
Must feel this way when they're transported home.
They step from the silver pod of the spaceship—
Home at last!—but why do the red canals
They once admired seem so appalling
With their electro-magnetic waves of dust?
The artificial lights that burn all night
In the cold caves beneath the arid surface
Hurt their tender eyes. But they adjust, I guess,
Learn to love again the hum of machinery
In the corridors beneath the raging dust storms,
And only at times, in small, windowless rooms,
When they look at their real faces in a mirror
To see the Martian wrinkles, dewlaps, baldness,
Do they remember the handsome, human faces
They wore on Earth—smooth lips, bright hair—
And feel nostalgia for a cloud or forest.

At my motel, I put my computer card
Into the lock and the door springs open.
The room is square and cool, one telephone
Beside my bed, another in the bathroom.
I open the blinds to see the parking lot
And beyond it—miles of brown on brown!
A lizard wrinkles through the blowing dust.
Lizards used to scurry through my yard
Ordinary as squirrels. How strange to forget
So many details I once took for granted—
The smell of creosote, the iron bars
Across the windows of the poorest houses,

The way I'd find a pregnant black widow
Nesting in my shoe, or under a lawn chair.
And know I had no choice, I had to kill.

Later, at the bar, I sit by the pool
Which curves indoors. I watch two swimmers stroke
From the glaring courtyard into the dark lounge.
They climb from the pool, silent, shivering,
Then plunge again into the aqua water.
I imagine living here as if I'd never left,
As if there were no Earth, no spring or fall.
I say words I haven't said in years:
"Mesquite," "Saguaro,"—and they burn my mouth
As if I'd eaten thorns.
I sip my salty drink, and tell myself,
Yes, this was home, this was a life I loved.

BELINDA SUBRAMAN

El Paso Sex

oil
refinery stink raging
in my nose
the fumes burn my eyes
you touch my breast
my sense refine
you kiss me
my head swells
1/4 mile from I-10
and the airport

the traffic
like fighter planes
persistent beyond anything
drives me mad
like your tongue
licking me just now

we close the windows
but it's too hot
we burn
the oil inside us
a fighter plane
hits its target

then the traffic
and the fumes
still stink

but in a charming way of course

H_2O

You speak of whale water
like a reborn sailor
with Cornish eyes
full of the wet dream.

I grew up on well water,
the wholesome underground.
The sea was a yearly visit,
a moving picture
that overwhelmed me.
I always came back

to what bodies need,
the purest source.

Will you ever love the subtle,
my little sighs
or the wetness
between my thighs?
I'm no ocean sailor
I'm water you dig for.

MARK WEBER

Hite Marina, Lake Powell

a fake lake
for phony people

no poetry
or sense of nature
having taken place

speedboats and waterskiers
screaming around
where Glen Canyon used to be

lost to us
in 1962

trash and debris along
the crippled shore

if you want to know more, read:
Jim Harrison's novel *A Good Day to Die*
and Edward Abbey's *The Monkey Wrench Gang*

we arrive here at dusk
only to catch a bathing swim
and pitch tent to rest
after all day hiking
Natural Bridges National Monument
investigating ancient injun sites

gone quick at sunrise.

CHARLOTTE M. WRIGHT

Polygamist

Picture this.
One stern patriarch, aged forty-three.
Wife the same.
Ten solid children at their side.

God says:
"Amos, take unto your bosom another wife."
Amos is startled.
"But God! I'm a poor man.
I have one house, two rooms, one wife, ten children.
One farm, and it a poor one.
Where, and how, and why . . . ?"
But God, he knows Amos.
Opens his eyes to the ways of the lord,
and those of one eighteen-year-old beauty.

Picture this, then.
An old wife, bitter and alone.
A hasty and secret ceremony.
One more cabin, two more rooms.
A young wife, wrapped in arms
the color and deadliness of hoarfrost.
Eventually, ten more children.

Polygamy was God's joke on them all.
It sent more people to hell,
than it did to heaven.

SOUTHERN
CALIFORNIA

CHRISTOPHER BUCKLEY

White

1964 and I'm parked
in my father's sports car
with Kathy Quigley,
it's late August
in Santa Barbara and
the moonsoaked foothills
simmer from the day's heat.
The top's down and finally,
without a word,
my hands sail
past the petticoat
and three clasps of the bra . . .
perspiration beads
on my clean-shaven lip,
the lemon blossoms
anoint the air;
we swear this is love
and burn beneath our stars.

◆

13 years and despite the loss
of orchards, the advance of homes,
kids still park out here
and throw their car doors open
to the high bleached grass of summer.
In an old Rambler
I light a cigarette
and wait for the moonrise
over La Cumbre Peak
like a host elevated by the priest
during Mass—I'd look for you then
amid a landscape of Catholic blouses . . .

And because my hands are blank
as this foothill shale,
because there is a moon,
I remember you
girl-like and eager as light.

Yet I'm content
without the life of averages
our parting spared me,
with whatever song
for my pockets month to month.
Tonight, under the stars
and all their thorns,
I no longer swear love
or know the misery—
I am blessed, purely
by the first memory
of your breasts,
by the simple grace
of what was here—
the lemon blossoms,
the white heart
of what we were.

CHARLES BUKOWSKI

from *Horsemeat*

V

my women of the past keep trying to locate me.
I duck into dark closets and pull the overcoats
about.

at the racetrack I sit in my clubhouse seat
smoking cigarette after cigarette
watching the horses come out for the post parade
and looking over my shoulder.

I go to bet—this one's ass looks like that one's
ass used to.
I duck away from her.

that one's hair might have her under it.
I get the hell out of the clubhouse and go
to the grandstand to bet.

I don't want a return of any of the past.
I don't want a return of any of those glorious
ladies of my past,
I don't want to try again, I don't want to see
them again even in silhouette;
I gave them all, gave all of them to all the other
men in the world, they can have the darlings,
the tits the asses the thighs the minds
and their mothers and fathers and sisters and
brothers and children and dogs and x-boy friends
and present boy friends, they can have them and
fuck them and hang them
upsidedown.

I was a terrible and a jealous man who mistreated
them and it's best that they are with you
for you will be better to them and I will be
better to myself
and when they phone me or write me or leave
messages
I will send them all to you
my fine fellows

I don't deserve what you have and I want to
keep it that way.

XX

20 minutes later
I had made my bets
and I walked out to the parking lot
and to my car.
I got in
opened the windows and
took off my shoes.

then I noticed
that I was blocked in.
some guy had parked behind me
in the exit space.

I started my engine
put it in reverse and
jammed my bumber against him.
he had his hand brake on
but luckily he was in neutral and
I slowly ground him back against
another car.
now the other car wouldn't be able
to get out.

what made a son-of-a-bitch
that way?
didn't they have any
consideration?

I put my shoes on
got out
and let the air out of his
left front tire.

no good.
he probably had a spare.
so I let the air out of his
left rear tire
got back into my car and
maneuvered it out of there
with some difficulty.

it felt good to
drive out of that racetrack.
it sure as hell felt better than
my first piece of ass and
many of the other pieces
which followed.

WANDA COLEMAN

Prisoner of Los Angeles (2)

in cold grey morning
comes the forlorn honk of workbound traffic
i wake to the video news report

the world is going off

rising, i struggle free of the quilt
& wet dreams of my lover dispel
leave me moist and wanting

in the bathroom
i rinse away illusions, brush my teeth and
unbraid my hair

there're the children to wake
breakfast to conjure
the job
the day laid out before me
the cold corpse of an endless grind

so this is it, i say to the enigma in the mirror
this is your lot/assignment/relegation
this is your city

i find my way to the picture window
my eyes capture the purple reach of hollywood's hills
the gold eye of sun mounting the east
the gray anguished arms of avenue

i will never leave here

The California Crack

she didn't know he was so shook

it started in his system/an erratic prance
some mechanism gone wet
codeine induced cellulitis, acid trails and flashes

he had nightmares about his mother pinching him in his
    sleep
his youth authority internment
the scar up his ass where they removed some thing
the lesbian he loved in Yucaipa
the black bird smashed against the window
of the stolen car

he began to sweat out his nights
when he woke his long dark brown hair was plastered
to his head. he was always dripping

it got so she couldn't stand laying next to him
the stench nauseated her, caused her to vomit
sometimes she made him sleep outside on the porch
so she could get an occasional night's rest
but most times she took breath by mouth

he went to the hospital
they took tests and found nothing
he went to the police
profuse sweating was not a crime
he took daily showers
the water bill went up
the seams in his clothes began to mold and erode
the sheets and comforter would not
wash clean

his septic sweat permeated everything
seeped down through the mattress into
the earth beneath their bed

one summer's midnight as they slept in his dampness
there was an earthquake
it measured 8.2 on the Richter scale
the bed split open the soft moist mouth of a scream
and she watched with mixed emotions
as he fell through

CHRIS DALY

the extras

all live in deck chairs on skid row
with their sunglasses and gucci carpetbags
in which they carry one once-decent jacket
or dress with all the stains and bare threads
on the back.

they all have their way with the camera.
one rolls his eyes back into his head, one
drapes a leg over her own neck, one makes
a funny motion with his cupped hand, one
swallows the tip of his nose. they develop
these tricks so the folks back home will
recognize them.

they love to laugh in a group but they live
to scream and shake their fists like an angry
mob.

traditionally, the lowest grade of cinema
fodder is given a substantial meal since it
may have to last a while. ratso would look
slow at an extra's buffet. spearchuckers have
been crushed diving for a box of chicken. if
shooting runs behind schedule the producers risk
a stampede of the star's steak & lobster wagon.

one occupational hazard: the slightest amount
of recognition is too much. one day you show
up and that smart bitch from casting informs
you that you stick out of a crowd.

so you shake hands all around though nobody
is shedding any tears and go back to the sub-
urbs where no one is very impressed and pick
up your life where you left it.

and now at the movies you watch the corner of the
screen and even in the parking lot you have an
extra's sense that all the world's a location.

no admittance

i was sitting in my taxi
reading the new york review of books.
i was saving the sports page for lunch
when i would be free from distraction.

when the words started running
to the right i folded that thing pronto.
one more run i was at the mexi joint,
no a/c but good food.

halfway through an enchilada a taco
beans rice and a salad the morning
briefing started going to the right
then to the left then straight up.

i threw some money on the table
and made it around the corner where
my cab was illegally parked in a driveway
across the sidewalk in front of a fire hydrant.

i got in and lay down except when
i was puking. i was surrounded by apt

buildings which blocked the wind &
decided my only chance was the park.

i barely made it, opened the door and
fell out on the grass. "look at that
cabbie! he's drunk on his ass!" i managed
to sit up and they kept going. then i went

down again. the radio was right there
but i opted for death if necessary
rather than ask the old prick dispatcher
for help. i guess i never admitted

i was a cabbie even when i was. somewhat
later without calling i headed for the
barn. twice on the way i had to stop and
hit the seat. i parked in a corner of

the yard reclined for an hour and somehow
managed to copy the tiny numbers off the
meter. then i made my move. i wasn't thinking
about getting inside for a cash drop,

i aimed for the chain link fence then my
car. i made it in one puke, lay down for
a while, then made the ten minute drive home
in 2-1/2 minute stretches, called in sick the

next day and by the following evening felt
just fine, though as a precaution i
eased up on the booze.

KEITH A. DODSON

Poor Losers

Authority is afraid
because for the first time
we have better guns
than they do
and if they
can't shoot first
and kill
then they have
nothing to keep us down.

They're worried
because the firepower
is in the streets
not in their pocket
and darkness
is scary
when you've lost control
and the masses
are beginning to think
for themselves
make decisions
for themselves
to organize
against those who've made
the rules
oppressive
to anyone outside the game
a game too few
are allowed to play
a game that is coming to an end

an end the politicians
don't like
an end the police
don't like because
their blood is being spilled
for a change
a game that is coming to an end
much sooner than they think
huddled behind their bureaucratic
attempts to change rules
in the middle
of
a game
they started.

MICHAEL C. FORD

The Disappearance of Deanna Durbin

I can understand the way it was with you,
Deanna!

One day, without any apparent warning,
Some neighbors we knew,
Without any warning, moved to
Costa Mesa, one day, where it was almost
As if they didn't have to watch, anymore,
A disintegration of dreamy conditions, as
Everything started to crumble in the soft
Dawn of disenchantment.

Why should they?
Like you, they were smart.

I didn't wise up, until much later!

What did you really do, Deanna?
Change your name?
Become a secret agent?
Do you ride the
Orient Express with the master plan in your pocket?
Are you bird-of-paradising it, like
Debra Paget all saronged and swooning,
While she tested the intentions of bristling boys
On the island?
Or, just like Joan Leslie, are you giving somebody
Enough faith in himself
To go up against the heaviest gunslinger on the
Jubilee Trail?
Or
Do you stand on the edge of a cliff
On foggy afternoons, waiting for a tanker that sank
Off the coast of Dover in 1941?

Do you sit, somewhere, in a sun-lit sanitarium
A beautiful and helpless amnesiac?

I bet you feel like St. Louis, when the
Brownies broke for Baltimore.

Maybe that's what broke your heart.

Well, Deanna, whatever you do, wherever you went,
This poem is just to say:
I'll be there in a minute!

ELLIOT FRIED

Campground

In the cool soft evening I lie on my trailer bed,
listening as the aluminum skin creaks, contracting
in the dusk. A few insects plink against the screen.

I get up, make coffee, listen to it bubbling
in its speckled pot. In the distance low voices
trickle from a tent swollen with yellow light.

I sit at the folding table, first pour coffee,
then Jack Daniels into a chipped enamel cup and drink.
The Winnebagos and Pace Arrows, mastodons,

have slouched into their slots, generators
silent. In this quiet time
the silhouettes of tamarisk and manzanita

fade and disappear. Here the wind breathes
a soft curtain of dust, skimming curlicues
from the road. An old man walks his dog . . .

his boots crunch on dry twigs. Finally,
near the gathering circles of fire, the campers
talk themselves mute, leaving only the crackling

of flame. Somewhere, whitewater thrashes
against stone. I lean my head against polished wood.
There is nothing left to do.

LISA GLATT

Hungry

Monday night. I'm at
Safeway. I feel
the honey dew and a man comes up, winks
at me with green eyes and walks away. I pick up
ears of corn and another man comes up
and asks about my melons. I don't quite understand
this influx of attention, having been a shopper
for years and never been approached. Suddenly I realize
it's "date night" and these shoppers
are tired of barstools, numb soles,
and vodka. These shoppers
buy their food for the week
on the night
the hungry
come
out

I leave with a guy
and a bottle of red wine. We go
to his apartment. The paint cracks
on all 4 walls. I comment
on his unfed plants. An insect
floats in a molded coffee cup and I'm happy here
in his mess
talking about toilet paper and garlic, unpacking his food
for the week. *People* magazine. He says he bought it
for the article on Bukowski. I tell him
he looks and walks like a writer. He shows me 4 poems.
3 are very good and I
kiss his cheek. We end up

rolling around on the bed. He tells me
he has only one ball.
I feel. Yes, one ball
but it's big. I show him
my scars and onions. He tells me
perfection is no great thing
and swallows my ear
like a vitamin.

DONNA HILBERT

Cerritos

To hide the cinder-block fence,
my husband and I plant bamboo
dug from the San Gabriel riverbed,
push sunflower seeds into old dairy
soil lightened with azalea mix,
scatter wildflower seeds over
the ground where sixty years ago
the Dutch brought their cows.

Across the street the county park lake
has become a stopping place
for migrating waterfowl.
Mergansers join abandoned
Easter ducks, mallards, and coots.
Cormorants fly in from the ocean,
dive for fish, stand one-legged
on the edge of the lake,
their black wings half-spread.

All the farms gone now,
Pete, an old dairy-man
fishes this lake every morning.
He says, "I hate those damn birds."
Then stands on one foot, arms
flailing for balance, and croons
like a cormorant—
a low, turkey-gobbling sound.

We are Dutch too. But so far back
what remains is just blondness
and our names. I think
we're here by accident. But, sometimes
I wonder if some ancestral force
pulled us to this lake,
this patch of suburb land.

Our neighbors tell us that bamboo
will over-run our lawn.
We are patient, sitting on damp
winter-yellow Bermuda, digging
into this ground, wondering who
thought to change the name
of our flat town from Dairy Valley
to "little mounds." We are patient,
listening for the dark warble
                            of the cormorant,
the distant lowing of cows.

KATHLEEN IDDINGS

Running Horse

In "76" I moved to California,
near pine bluffs and arroyos
on sacred land of the Digueños.
My neighbor Running Horse, braided and serene,
grew up on a reservation.

Says when he was six his father took him to a dime store—
held up item after item saying incredulously,
"This is crazy."
Looked quietly in his son's eyes and said,
"Please don't get crazy."

Running Horse and I watch nearby bulldozers
flatten bluffs for condo cities,
bury sage and manzanita forever.
He shakes his head and says quietly,
"This is crazy."

MARAEL JOHNSON

Systems Alert

Michael wants to
make up for postponing
our fifteenth anniversary,

a day he spent
with his old Volvo
at Keith's Auto Electric.
The urgent problem?
A dead battery
and warning lights
that flashed red.
He promises
a planned
bus tour
through Europe
so I won't
have to worry
about a thing.
He offers this to me—
a live wire who
circuits the globe
alone,
sparks missions,
charges frontiers
and pees along
roadsides.
He offers this to me—
whom he met hitchhiking
in Sweden, about
the same time
his car was built.
His priority was
well-taken because,
unlike the Volvo,
I'm still putting out
plenty of juice
and can quit
with no warning.

269   SOUTHERN CALIFORNIA

MARILYN JOHNSON

Our Mothers Were Sisters

Now the riverbed is lined with concrete.
The banks are geometric slopes.
The water no longer meanders
but flows down a shallow slot
dead center in the floor.
The trees are gone.
The floods are gone.
But I know the concrete wasn't always there
paving the place where I could also be Richard.

Together, we would crawl under the chainlink fence
and slide down the hard dirt slope to the sand.
Beneath the pillar of the bridge,
engraved with our favorite graffiti—
"To hell with the parade,
let's go watch the elephants fuck"—
we would talk about things
like the dream of how it feels to fly,
when gravity disappears
like a slow motion movie.

Our mothers were sisters,
but that night they locked me out of the room.
I cried because I wanted to settle down
in the water with you,
in the tub with the claw feet,
to feel your skin slippery with soap
in that room that smelled of the pink oval
wired to the inside of the toilet.
But they locked me out.

I was no longer allowed to touch you
or sleep in the same bed with you.
And when they finally told you
that your mother had gone insane
you ran away without me
to eat oranges
stolen from the groves along the river.

RON KOERTGE

Redondo

Beneath my feet the pier shifts
and drools. Above, some gulls carve
out the sturdy air as surfers arrange
themselves like quarter notes across
a distant wave.

It is a relief to stop staring at girls,
to quiet the heart's thick strokes
and calmly pass the man with a truant
officer's soft chest and scowl, a boy
writing a post card—that small hymn—
staring at the pictured sand he is sunk
in, even the great great grandchildren
of Lady Macbeth washing their hands
again and again at the edge
of the unraveling world

What a place to have God rear his
amazing head. Yet here I am, all

the clutter inside made in your image.
The ocean is forever changing its clothes
to be more beautiful for you. There
is the horizon which you have drawn
with a golden rule and outlined, too,
a tiny ship and curl of smoke to make
the scene complete.

Blue

The pornographer changes sheets,
tucks in a fitted bottom, turns back
the top, sighs.

"This is a threesome," he says, "so
it's you over here, Suzanne. You down
there, Billy. And Monica, wherever,
okay?

It's pretty early, but they try hard.
Once this was risky: cops and reporters
everywhere. Now it pays the bills,

though on a good day it can be a
counter-spell to all the sick and unjust
things in the world

and every now and then it's really
lovely, one of those kindnesses
nobody understands.

Dear Superman

I know you think that things
will always be the same: I'll rinse
out your tights, kiss you goodbye
at the window and every few weeks
get kidnapped by some stellar goons.

But I'm not getting any younger
and you're not getting any older.
Pretty soon I'll be too frail
to take aloft, and with all those
nick-of-time rescues you're bound
to pick up somebody more tender
and just as ga-ga as I used to be.
I'd hate her for being 17 and you
for being . . . what, 700?

I can see your sweet face as you read
this and I know you'd like to siphon
off some strength for me, even if it
meant you could only leap small buildings
at a single bound. But you can't
and, anyway, would I want to
just stand there while everything
else rushed past?

Take care of yourself and of the world
which is your own true love. One day
soon as you patrol the curved earth,
that'll be me down there tucked in
for good being what you'll never be
but still

Your friend,

Lois Lane

STEVE KOWIT

Josephine's Garden

First thing in the morning
the phone rings. It's Mary
to tell me that Jack,
after two years with AIDS,
has finally died.
An hour later the ophthalmologist
puts some sort of drops in my eyes
& for the rest of the day the light is blinding.
When I go outside I have to wear
those dark paper shades the nurse gave me—
even the pulpy grey stones
& the faded hedge & the pale
green spikes of the barrel cactus
in Josephine's garden
are too bright to look at,
while her roses & bougainvillea
blaze out as if someone had suddenly
flung back the shutters—
as blinding as one of those
high-mountain blizzards,
but more gorgeous
& painful.
If this is the way the world really is
it's too much to look at.
No one could ever survive it.
Nevertheless, all afternoon,
I keep stepping out into that garden,
eyes smarting as if someone
had rinsed them in acid. Astonished
again at the unbelievable colors.
The utter profusion of forms.
The sharp edges everything has in this world.

LA LOCA

from *Adventures on the Isle*
of Adolescence

Hello, animal sacrifice hotline?
Do you incinerate teenage boys?
Here they come
The Swarm
Hear the drone of their skateboards
As they approach
like an armada
and run
for cover of the nearest sleazy bar
where they check I.D.
and have bouncers like rhinoceri
Secrete thyself on the furthest stool
Shield thyself with a vodka martini
and wait till the air raid siren ceases.
17 years ago
polite company
screwed on hallucinogens
with the intent to produce
offspring which would be
trippy.
This coup of genetic engineering—
enacted at Be-ins, under bushes, on acid—
was to be the Aquarian gift to the race.
After all, by 1961
God's remains had been discovered in a
tar pit by the County Museum.
He was dead.
Laboratories were Lord
and Chemistry was Life.
Junkies and alkies slouched the earth

Supreme.
And the brain damaged naturally selected the
brain damaged
and they were born
incubated on fungus and fry
yanked from the host
buzzed like a saw.
The Scions of Altered Consciousness.
The New Breed

◆ ◆ ◆

The pack veering toward me in formation
like I'm quarry.
I'll just keep walking down the sidewalk
like I don't notice
the juggernaut of testosterone
mowing me down.
I grip my purse to me, tight
with the angst that only those in
majority can know and
I pray to the God who was reinstated
in 1979:
Please
let this be the primarily peyote-gestated branch
which rarely bites
Please
let them be crocked on
popsicles, Coors and cheap Mexican weed
Please, please
just let me get to the end of the block
without getting a chunk of my butt
tweaked by a twit
and they thrash by
thunderous
in a deafening brouhaha

with a mighty "fuck this" and
a mighty "fuck that"

♦ ♦ ♦

Fuck everybody everywhere in the world
all the time for any reason.
A congested aggregate of gnats
dense with fuck
and they slalom around me
and I only get goosed once.
Thank you God.
There is a God.
I take a deep breath.

D. H. LLOYD

Bible Bob Responds to a Jesus Honker

On the way home from the University, I saw
Bible Bob driving the car ahead of me. He had
A bumper sticker that said, "Honk if you
Love Jesus." Not having much hate for anyone,
Expecially Jesus, I tooted my horn twice.
Bible Bob jabbed his left hand out the open
Window, Raised his middle finger in salute
To me and shouted,
"What the hell's your damned hurry, buddy?"

GERALD LOCKLIN

california

what the hell am i doing anyway?
i mean, my eyes are photo-sensitive,
i'm scared of big waves, and sweating in the sand
bores the knickers off me. furthermore,

i am not exactly mr. abdominal
definition of southern california.
i compensate, however, by being mr.
inarticulate (what do you say

to these blithely dispirited bodies, when
you can't tell whether they're fifteen or
thirty-five and, back home, even the ugly ones
cried rape if you so much as tipped your cap?)

of course, the beach has its moments, like parked
above the phosphorescent scaly tide
at sunset, and the girl will blossom soon,
her nipples gone dusk red, into a young woman.

even here, though, peril. only once i
tried to make it on the shore, and it
was sand up in her crotch, my crevices,
a cold wind howling at my asshole, my

corrugated knees kept sliding out
from under me, and then i lost my glasses
and my credit cards, scuttling like t.s. eliot
in flotsam and jetsam, whichever is which

never again. nor disneyland either,
although it was free and with the girl i love.

the lines are long, the rides aren't scary, people
seem to think they have fun, like

when the whole country jerked off over the moonshot.
no, and i don't want to go to marineland,
let alone busch gardens or universal stupidos.
for all of me, the queen mary could sink.

i do like rooting for the rams though, and
the lakers; i like a big league town.
and the girls don't have legs like farmers,
and it *is* the biggest ocean.

the food is the worst imaginable,
but there are all kinds of movies playing.
there are curiosities like the gay bars;
might as well be where it happens first.

well, the discussion is no doubt academic,
since we're all dying of emphysema.
as grandma always used to say: you made
your oyster bed, now grovel in it.

a constituency of dunces

"you know," lara says,
"adrienne rich can always count on
five hundred feminists showing up
for her readings."

and amiri baraka and ishmael reed
can count on the blacks.

and politically involved readers
will flock to hear carolyn forche,

and bob and dennis draw the gays.

and gary soto the chicanos.

and ferlinghetti and levertov
have fame and politics both:

i mean, it's not that these writers can't write—
i just mean that they also have their followings
that they can count on."

"where's mine?" i ask.

"your problem," she says, "is that the people
to whom your work might appeal
do not read poetry.
in fact, most of those
who might share your attitudes or viewpoint

either don't or can't read at all."

NICHOLA MANNING

Three Cars

The three cars covered three
small, roving rectangles
of Earth, but they were
handsome, brightly painted

and clean—and so had airs
of importance, important
destinations. One was
about to be stripped

in a junkyard. The second
was a new arrival to the dry
L.A. river bed. And the
third was falling from the

top of a San Pedro cliff.

LIZBETH PARKER

A Girl My Age

Toward the end of my
fourteenth summer,
lying in my
San Fernando bedroom,
I wrote a story
of a girl my age
who lived on a prairie farm
and waited through
the ceaselessly hot summer
for rain. It was

very dramatic, filled
with dire
needs for rain:
thirsty animals,

soon-to-be-failed crops,
ever present dust.
The girl lay awake nightly
listening to the
absence of rain.
Finally, of course,
the rain came. I described

the pud-puff of raindrops
lifting the dust, the
breeze that gave
breath to the curtains,
and the girl
inhaling repeatedly
to store within herself
the aroma of rain first
dampening the earth. Oh

Joyful Rain. Oh Saving Rain.
It was a terrible story. I
knew nothing of the prairie.
But I thought no one
would believe that I,
who lived surrounded
by groves of other
people's trees force-fed
through horse-neck pipes,
could so desperately
need the rain.

ROBERT PETERS

Hollywood Boulevard Cemetery

I recall Ty Power's beauty:
his slender waist,
his black eyes—as he appeared
as Prince Rudolph in *Thin Ice*
with Sonja Henie.

I ask Mitchum to kneel and kiss
the tiny Greek-temple monument.

I pluck a tulip from an urn
and jab it into Mitchum's lapel.

"Let's vamoose," he says.
"The Busby Berkeley girls are coming.
They'll chop us to pieces with their heels."

True, I hear the clicks
of a thousand stilettos beneath the sod.

Then a heart-beat, a few graves over
from Ty's. It's Nelson Eddy
preparing to sing "Indian Love Call."

BRENT REITEN

Sex with Zsa Zsa and Eva Gabor

They were trying to put their poodles
into the back of a limo.
I was talking to a Watchtower woman
in front of Woolworth's.
One said, Vell, are you just
going to stand there and vatch?
I said, Excuse me?

Inside, in the back of the limo,
one said, Dahling, have you ever seen
two prettier dogs in your life?
The other said, Come over here
vhere you can pet them.
She said, They von't bite.

Down 27th Avenue, on the way to wherever,
one took the Watchtower from my hand,
the other the shirt off my back.
One said, Daddy taught us not to be greedy.
The other said, Daddy taught us to share.

I was sandwiched between them,
an albino Oreo of unknown consequences.
One said, Have you ever licked
prettier titties? The other said,
Have you ever been licked by prettier ladies?

We are driving along wherever.
The car was rocking like a cradle.
One said, Let the dogs do vhat they vant.
The other said, They're our little dahlings, too.

On the street, back in front of Woolworth's,
I fell into the arms of the Watchtower woman.
I said, I don't know if I'm man, dog or child.

She said, it doesn't matter what you are.
She said, The Armageddon's on its way.
She said, Just be Jehovah's witness.
She said, Just watch it all go down,

with us.

JOAN JOBE SMITH

Heartthrobs

My Aunt Louise subscribed to *Photoplay*,
wrote fan letters, and kept a movie star
scrapbook for so long that she began to
hallucinate. Boldfaced lie, my father said,
but I believed my Aunt Louise's story that
the movie star Richard Egan had fallen
head-over-heels in love with her, drove
all the way from Hollywood to Colton,
California, to meet her Saturday afternoons
at the chili dog stand on Mt. Vernon Boulevard.
Just to hold her hand, nothing else,
my Aunt Louise, only 16, swore to her daddy,
a hot-headed Texas railroad man, who got out
his pistol and cleaned it and loaded it and
tried to sneak up on Richard Egan at the
chili dog stand to catch him in the act
with his little girl. But he always
got there too late, Richard Egan just

having driven away, just moments before,
back to L.A. in his red '54 Coupe de Ville.
Someday, someday, my grandpa would say,
I'm gonna get me that slippery son of a bitch,
and my father would say, Jesus Christ, if this
don't beat all, and go outside to grind his teeth.
Later, on our way back home to Long Beach
my father'd say if Louise were his girl,
teen-ager or not, he'd get out his belt and
wallop some sense into her butt, and I
knew that he would, so I never told him when
Robert Wagner began peeking into my
bedroom window on nights the moon was full.

Me and My Mother's Morphine

Deukmejian and the DEA, my mother's doctor
says, keep close tabs on Californians'
medical morphine use, so I must drive
five miles once a week to fetch in person
The Triplicate, a beige, crisp piece of
paper, as dear as a cashier's check, to
take five miles the other side of town to
the only pharmacy that carries my mother's
liquid morphine. On the way, I stop at
Trader Joe's for mine, the California kind:
green syringes of sauvignon blanc, chablis,
chardonnay, Sebastiani Eye of the Swan I
later sip from a plastic cup to blur
Life while I spoonfeed my bedridden mother
her supper.

"Now I know why you drink wine," she says,
a teetotaler, a good Christian woman who's
never approved of my drinking. "Being
doped up brings you closer to God," she
says, seeing Sistine things now upon
her ceiling, fidgeting and licking her
lips, the one-half cubic centimeter of
morphine, the same color blue as Windex.
I give her mornings and bedtime in apple
juice more potent to her 70 pounds than
a $100 heroin hit to a prickled L.A. hype.

Sad and ashamed of her addiction as much
as her disease, sometimes she weeps as she
sucks through a straw the last drop of
morphine from the cup, and sometimes I
imagine Deukmejian and the DEA boys breaking
down my mother's bedroom door—conquistadores
roaring "Eureka!"—coming to prick their
spears at us, a couple pagans all right,
red-eyed and doped-up, naked with sin
and death.

TIMOTHY STEELE

A Shore

It's pastoral enough—the flat, slick sand;
The towel draped round the neck, as if a yoke;
The toppling waves; the sunset, as it smoulders
And drains horizonwards, fiery, baroque;

The young girl sitting on her father's shoulders
Directing his attention here and there,
Her ankles held and her unpointing hand
Contriving a loose pommel of his hair.

Here strollers pass, pant legs rolled up like sleeves,
Shoes hanging over shoulders, laces tied,
While godwits—rapier bills upcurved—peruse
Bubbles beneath which burrowed sand crabs hide.
Though hardly anyone these days conceives
That this is where the known meets the unknown,
The ocean still transmits its cryptic news
By means of a conch's ancient cordless phone.

And night will put an end to pastorals.
A crescent moon will cup its darker sphere.
The waves will crash in foam and flood up through
The forest of the piles below the pier.
Alone, archaically, the sea will brew
Its sundry violence beyond the shore,
Beyond the sweeping beam, where heaving swells
Of kelp-beds wage titanic tugs-of-war.

CHARLES STETLER

To John Garfield, for Whom
the Postman Only Rang Once

No one knows why you killed yourself,
but your movies offer clues.
You snapped everything:
cigarette cases, hat brims, gloves, women.

In comparison, Britain's Angry Young Men
were honor roll students from Dale Carnegie.
You were representative, but I'm not sure of what.
A lost generation of one, in boxing gloves or
                             pinstripe suits.
As the honest crook in *Force of Evil,* you told
                             Eleanor Parker:
"My trouble is I feel like midnight."

Mostly though you spat out words
except at types like Priscilla Lane.
Robert Blake swears you saved the fragments of his
                             childhood sanity
fathering him while he played your younger self in
                             Humoresque.

Like most tragic figures, you left heavy prints.
Nick Adams patterned himself after you even in death.
But Lilli Palmer summed you up most complexly
when she cooed at the confused, scar-tissued
                             welterweight:
"Tyger! tyger! burning bright,
in the forest of the night."

"What's that mean?" you asked.
Stroking your tired but still tight bicep,
she murmured: "Well built."

You had to be sad and lonely,
but we loved you, if not only,
we loved you, body and soul.

hit in the head

in the men's room on upper campus
the newly installed, AIDS inspired
condom machine had been wrenched open,
its front panel flapping
like a prudish tongue.
the cupboard was bare.

what sexual Ahab frenzy had
stirred this King Kong passion?

did the hot, little number in Anthro I
whisper in his ear after a Dionysian
slide presentation on pagan rites:
"After class tonight, in your van,
but only if you have a you-know-what."

was the football squad's defensive team
invited to an impromptu first victory bash
after six losses into the new season?

was a diseased victim trying to deliver
a message, make contact, so to speak?

was this merely the mundane, imagineless
result of frat fellows on a scavenger search?

let us hope for some romance here.

perhaps our Hero inflated a few of the leftovers
to buoy him on his return across the Hellespont
after leaving lovely Leander thoroughly sated.

PAUL TRACHTENBERG

Laguna

I flew to Laguna
in my fiery Impala.
I landed by the soupy sea
with those shrieks
serenading me.

I dabbled in dope
and looked into a kaleidoscope.
My muscles kept that summer suspended.

Mystic Craze

There was something cozy
about this realm—a poet
in a purple jungle;
creatures hula-hooping
or dancing a passacaglia.

I was on the crest, ready
to kick out, taking a left side.
Grabbin' the rail, I avoided
the curling wave.

FRED VOSS

Edgy

Having worked from 12 midnight to 6:58 A.M.,
the graveyard shift machinist
seems too awake,
his face twitching with tics and giggles
as his eyes dart about
and he tries to sweep up the aluminum chips
on the floor around his machine,
striking out violently with his pushbroom
in a chaos of changing directions,
the keys on his belt slapping against his butt.
Finally he is snapping shut his toolbox and
        heading out the door
for the bar
as the sun comes up.
Drunk by noon,
he will be driving
to the racetrack or the beach
with a cooler full of beer
as he tries to stave off
that nervous breakdown
that has claimed so many of his fellow
graveyard machinists.

The Stud

He had worked out at Gold's Gym
until he could bench-press 450 pounds.

He walked around the machine shop
waving a 50-pound lead hammer above his head

with one hand,
and his hammer blows
echoed off the machine shop walls
like gunshots.

Then he started talking
about how much he liked to fuck
his boyfriend.

For the first time in the machine shop's 20-year history,
no one was telling any faggot jokes.

Lingo

After years and years in machine shops,
machinists begin to talk less and less.
Instead, they begin to
tap their rubber or lead or ball-peen hammers
against their machines,
learning how to play their machines like steel drums.
They walk around with big sheets of sheet metal,
bending and buckling them
until they whirr and hum
like weird high-tech
guitar solos.
They line up cutter holders of varying diameters
and play them like organ pipes
by sticking the tips of their airguns into them
and blasting air through them,
or they blast air against the insides of their closed
fists and create kazoo-like sounds
by rubbing and opening and closing their fingers
and thumbs—

until occasionally, when they are really inspired,
they break out in vocals
to lead their own one-man bands—
the Italians singing opera,
the Mexicans mariachi,
and the bikers
heavy metal.

CHARLES WEBB

Dr. Invisible and Mr. Hide

for Ron Koertge

Like a low tide, the Malibu girl's
green bikini bottom has rolled back,
exposing white crescents above her legs'
tan-line. Her bra-straps lie, spread wide
as handlebars, beside her on the sand,
cups peeling down from breasts as white
and curved and smooth as ostrich eggs.

"I'd like to hide in the girls' locker
room," I say. "And watch her change."
"Yeah," says Ron. "Or be invisible
and follow her home." While our peers
plod through the sad tome *Middle Age,*
we prowl L.A., and dream of roaming
unseen through showers and bedrooms,
crouching behind the doctor's screen
at the Clinic for Young Actresses & Models,
slipping backstage at the Bikini Festival,
our eyes, like God's, everywhere.

As younger guys belabor wills
and brace to die, Ron and I feed
raw flesh to the boys alive and well
inside us, the same boys who risked
buckshot and juvie hall to peer
through neighbors' blinds at panty-
girdles, slips, and see-through bras.

What, after all, is growing old
but ceasing to desire? What
is death but hiding underground,
a sure-fire way to be invisible?
A thousand years from now
as some tan angel steps into
her bath and drops her towel,
don't be surprised if the soap
whispers, "Charlie—I'm in heaven,"
and the steam replies "I know,
Ron, I'm right here with you."

JILL YOUNG

The Light That Made Him Whisper

A lisp of death was always on my father's lips.
For this and other reasons I loved him.
He had a sense of twilight.
We lived in a city of bowling alleys
and stucco tract houses
with patchy lawns and no sidewalks.
And all of it looked so ugly

under the modern California sun.
But we would go to the antique shops,
pick our way through
the dim clutter
of wardrobes that still smelled of their people
and sour perfume
and beds where he told me people
had been birthed
and people had died.
Cut glass the colors of melted ices,
green and violet,
lined the windows of these places,
cast jagged crosses of light
onto the deep afternoon of the walls.
The light made him whisper.
"Ah my green and blue beauties,"
he would say, speaking to the glass
so only I could hear him.
I remember garlands of women's hair,
russet and black,
blond that had faded to the color
of old sheets,
and I would think of the women in the Victorian
    engravings
with their hair tumbling to their knees
and their lips drawn together
like sections of tiny oranges, smiling.
And in those beds he pointed to,
I knew women had died,
bled to death,
and I could imagine the smell of warm blood
soaking their white peignoirs
and the feeble babies mewing
in their languid arms.
"Judith," he said one day as we walked
through a field of chairs.

"We almost named you Judith."
He told me about her,
a little girl
who died when she was three,
back somewhere in my grandmother's girlhood.
And I thought of that girl
dying when she was a year younger
than myself,
and of the last century
which in my brain hovered
like a grove of light-spattered pepper trees,
and of her little coffin,
and of all the beautiful, dying women
with names like waltzes.

RAFAEL ZEPEDA

Cowboys and Indians

Jose cruises Watts in his '74 chevy coupe that's lowered
to the ground and painted burgundy. The other night he
told me that he was going to buy some new rims.
"It's good deal," he said. "My rims and fifty dollars."
"What's wrong with the old rims?" I asked.
"Nothing," he said. "But these rims are better.
I got to be absent tomorrow."
"To get the rims?"
"Yeah," he said and smiled.
That was too bad, since Jose was often the only student
to come to class.

But a couple of nights later he came back. It was
raining, the wind pushing the rain inland.
"Did you get them?" I asked.
"Yeah," he said. "Want to see them?"
"Sure," I said.
"I think the mayates want to get them."
"Not in the rain," I said.
We went out to the parking lot where the chevy was parked
under a light. The rain was beading up on the wax, the
rims were shining. A couple of black students stood under
a tree. They smoked cigarettes
and talked.
"Nice rims," I said.
"Those fucking mayates," Jose said.
"What?"
"Didn't you hear those guys?"
"Nope," I said.
"They want to get my rims. Didn't you hear them?"
"What did you get them for? Around here nothing's safe."
"I have to have something," he said. "Those fucking
mayates.
They think I'm stupid."
We went back inside, out of the rain.

I haven't seen Jose for a while since then. Antonio, a
guy from Salvador, said a guy with a rifle was chasing
him the last time that he saw him.
"Why's that?" I asked.
"I don't know." Antonio shrugged.
"I think they like those rims."

Burrito

My brother and I delivered flowers
for my father for years.
We drove all over L.A.
from Long Beach to Gardena
to Pico Riverato Whittier
Hollywood to Central L.A.
And we never had time to
stop and eat anything
but burritos that we could
grab and take with us
down the road.
So we gained a facility for
picking burrito stands that
were good on sight.
They usually had a sign
painted green and red and yellow
that had been done by a novice.
And they usually had a couple of
people standing around, Mexicans
and maybe a couple of Blacks.
When we got closer
there was always that menu
that was in Spanish
that reassured us that
this was a good place
for a red chile or green chile
burrito that we could take
to fill us and drip in our laps
as we took the flowers to funeral
parlor, hospital, birthday girl,
or lover.
We with our full stomachs.
They with their sadness, recuperation,
happiness, or love pangs.

The Wreckers

At night they cross the border,
brown men in brown trucks
with brown windows.
They are covered with dust.
Their diesel puffs behind them.
And it is strange that their
white license plates say
FRONT on the front
and FRONT on the back.
Just before dawn they find the
old buildings. The doors open,
the brown men get out,
crow bars in their right hands,
hammers at their sides.
Behind them comes a hunchback
with the sledge hammers.

I watched them take Beacon Street
in Pedro, the old Long Beach Municipal.
I watched them take Spanish Mansions from
along the ocean, and one place that
some Bauhaus guy probably designed.
They take the chrome rails, the fixtures,
the doors, the plumbing, the bricks
and all the big lumber. The supports.
They rip up the plaster, the dust rising.
They gut the places and knock them down;
then there's an empty dirt lot,
high rise material.

But now I have the feeling
that one day
I will go south

to the land of the quetzal bird
and there they'll be
the old building that they took,
Beacon Street set up along the coast
at the Sea of Cortez Historical Museum,
and the old Municipal,
renowned for when the Band played there,
alongside of it.
The mansions and the chrome-covered buildings.
Everything.
Because they're taking things back,
piece by piece.
Taking California, Arizona, New Mexico, Texas,
Nevada, Colorado and Utah.
As much as they can get.
And one day they'll have it all
down there.

A. ZOLYNAS

Considering the Accordion

The idea of it is distasteful at best. Awkward box of wind, diminutive, misplaced piano on one side, raised braille buttons on the other. The bellows, like some parody of breathing, like some medical apparatus from a victorian sick-ward. A grotesque poem in three dimensions, a rococo thing-am-a-bob. I once strapped an accordion on my chest and right away I had to lean back on my heels, my chin in the air, my back arched like a bullfighter or flamenco dancer. I became an unheard of contradiction:

a gypsy in graduate school. Ah, but for all that, we find
evidence of the soul in the most unlikely places. Once in
a Czech restaurant in Long Beach, an ancient accordion-
ist came to our table and played the old favorites: "Lady
of Spain," "The Sabre Dance," "Dark Eyes," and through
all the cliches his spirit sang clearly. It seemed like the
accordion floated in air, and he swayed weightlessly
behind it, eyes closed, back in Prague or some lost village
of his childhood. For a moment we all floated—the whole
restaurant: the patrons, the knives and forks, the wine,
the sacrificed fish on plates. Everything was pure and
eternal, fragiley suspended like a stained-glass window in
the one remaining wall of a bombed out church.

The Man Who Had Singing Fits

He would begin unexpectedly anywhere,
bubbling into song at the Woolworth's cash register,
in the elevator, in the restaurant
as the waitress approached with coffee,
in board meetings.

The pale canary of his heart chirped
from its cage while all around him
we woke momentarily, startled
out of our cultural trance,
too amazed to be embarrassed.

His family and friends were used to these fits,
and we too became charmed
by his soft voice, the lilting, gentle song

that never quite made sense
but had something to do
with a quiet, confused love.

He would sing for a half minute,
and then he'd be back among us, no memory
of his departure or return, no memory
of the stream he'd dipped us all into,
that one running along just under
the surface of anything you and I
think we understand.

Found Poem

after information received
in The St. Louis Post-Dispatch,
4 v 86

The population center of the USA
Has shifted to Potosi, in Missouri.

The calculation employed by authorities
In arriving at this dislocation assumes

That the country is a geometric plane,
Perfectly flat, and that every citizen,

Including those in Alaska and Hawaii
And the District of Columbia, weighs the same;

So that, given these simple presuppositions,
The entire bulk and spread of all the people

Should theoretically balance on the point
Of a needle under Potosi in Missouri

Where no one is residing nowadays
But the watchman over an abandoned mine

Whence the company got the lead out and left.
"It gets pretty lonely here," he says, "at night."

Howard Nemerov

ACKNOWLEDGMENTS

Kim Addonizio: "The Philosopher's Club," first published in *The Threepenny Review.* Reprinted by permission of the author.

Elizabeth Alexander: "West Indian Primer" and "A Poem for Nelson Mandela" from *The Venus Hottentot* by Elizabeth Alexander. Reprinted by permission of The University Press of Virginia.

Jack Anderson: This section of "Field Trips on the Rapid Transit" from *Field Trips on the Rapid Transit,* published by The University of Pittsburgh Press, is reprinted by permission of the author.

Antler: "The Discovery of Lake Michigan" is used by permission of the author.

Amiri Baraka: This excerpt from "A Poem of Destiny" is used by permission of the author.

Jim Barnes: "An Ex-Deputy Sheriff Remembers the Eastern Oklahoma Murderers: i. Summerfield ii. Red Oak" is used by permission of the author.

Gerald Barrax: "Spirituals, Gospels" is used by permission of the author.

John Bensko: "The Wild Horses of Assateague Island" first appeared in *Poetry.* Reprinted by permission of the author.

David Bergman: "Urban Renewal, Baltimore" is used by permission of the author.

Sallie Bingham: "Two Girls" is used by permission of the author.

David Bottoms: "Face Jugs: Homage to Lanier Meaders" and "The Window" are used by permission of the author.

James Broughton: "Aglow in Nowhere" is used by permission of the author.

Christopher Buckley: "White" is used by permission of the author.

Charles Bukowski: Sections V and XX from "Horsemeat," ©

Toi Derricotte: "Blackbottom" is used by permission of the author.

John DeWitt: "Old Post Grill" is used by permission of the author.

James Dickey: "Root-light, or the Lawyer's Daughter" is used by permission of the author.

Patricia Dobler: "Field Trip to the Rolling Mill, 1950," reprinted from *Talking to Strangers*, by Patricia Dobler, © 1986, published by the University of Wisconsin Press. Used by permission of the publisher.

Keith A. Dodson: "Poor Losers" is used by permission of the author.

Sharon Doubiago: "Signal Hill" is used by permission of the author.

Barbara Drake: "When the Airplane Stopped" and "Mother Said" were first published in *What We Say to Strangers* (Breitenbush Publications, 1986). Reprinted by permission of the author.

Stephen Dunn: "Walking the Marshland" is reprinted from *Between Angels, Poems* by Stephen Dunn, by permission of the author and W.W. Norton & Company, Inc. Copyright © 1989 by Stephen Dunn. "At the Smithville Methodist Church" is reprinted from *Local Time*, published by William Morrow & Company, Inc., by permission of the publisher. © Copyright by Stephen Dunn, 1986.

Cornelius Eady: "Atomic Prayer" is used by permission of the author.

Martin Espada: "Trumpets from the Islands of Their Eviction" is reprinted from *Trumpets from the Islands of their Eviction* by Martin Espada, with permission of the publisher, Bilingual Press/Editorial Bilingüe, Arizona State University, Tempe, AZ. © Copyright 1987 by Bilingual Press/Editorial Bilingüe.

Lawrence Ferlinghetti: This section of "The Old Italians Dying" is used by permission of the author.

Edward Field: "The Last Bohemians" is used by permission of the author.

Steve Fisher: "Weather Nose" is used by permission of the author.

Michael C. Ford: "The Disappearance of Deanna Durbin" is used by permission of the author.

Charles Fort: "The Worker (We Own Two Houses)" first

appeared in *The Town Clock Burning*, published by St. Andrew's Press, 1985, and is used by permission of the author.

Elliot Fried: "Campground" is used by permission of the author.

Tess Gallagher: "Black Money" copyright 1976 by Tess Gallagher. Reprinted from *Instuctions to the Double*. "Legend with Sea Breeze" copyright by Tess Gallagher. Reprinted from *Moon Crossing Bridge*, both with the permission of Greywolf Press, St. Paul, Minnesota.

George Garrett: "Long & Short of It: A Letter to Brendan Galvin" is used by permission of the author.

Charles Ghigna: "The Untold Truth about Hank" is used by permission of the author.

Gary Gildner: "The Porch" is used by permission of the author.

Allen Ginsberg: "Velocity of Money" is used by permission of the author.

Jon Forrest Glade: "Sex Education," "The Weight of the Sheets," and "Blood Trail" are used by permission of the author.

Lisa Glatt: "Hungry" first appeared in Genre, published at California State University, Long Beach, and is used by permission of the author.

Robert Glück: "The Chronicle" was first published in *Reader* by The Lapis Press, © 1988. Reprinted by permission of the author.

Laurence Goldstein: "Ann Arbor Solitary" is used by permission of the author.

Jim Gove: "Meditating at Olema" is used by permission of the author.

Arthur Gregor: "Gentle Lamb" first appeared in *The New Yorker* and is used by permission of the author.

Jim Gustafson: "The Idea of Detroit" was published in *Shameless* (Toumbuctu, 1978) and is reprinted by permission of the author.

R. S. Gwynn: "A Short History of the New South" is reprinted from *The Drive-In: Poems* by R. S. Gwynn, used by permission of the University of Missouri Press. Copyright 1986 by the author.

Marilyn Hacker: "Runaways Café I" is used by permission of the author.

Jana Harris: "We Fish Our Lives Out" and "Norma at the A&W Drive-In" first appeared in *The Clackamas* (The Smith, New York, 1979) and are used by permission of the author.

Robert Hass: "Name as the Shadow of the Predator's Wing" and "Adhesive: For Earlene" are used by permission of the author.

Hunt Hawkins: "Mourning the Dying American Female Names"

first appeared in *The Southern Review* and is used by permission of the author.

Michael Heffernan: "Living Room" is used by permission of the author.

Donna Hilbert: "Cerritos" is used by permission of the author.

Anselm Hollo: "In the Land of Art" first appeared in *Outlying Districts* by Anselm Hollo (Coffee House Press, 1990). Reprinted by permission of the publisher. Copyright © 1990 by Anselm Hollo.

Christopher Howell: "Mean and Stupid" first appeared in *The Mid-West Quarterly* and is used by permission of the author.

Harry Humes: "My Mother at Evening" first appeared in *Raccoon* and then in *The Way Winter Works*, published by The University of Arkansas Press. © 1990 by Harry Humes.

Kathleen Iddings: "Running Horse" first appeared in *Selected and New Poems, 1980-1990*, by Kathleen Iddings, copyright 1990, published by West Anglia Publications, Box 2683, La Jolla, CA 92038.

Manuel Igrejas: "Herois do Mar" is used by permission of the author.

Lorri Jackson: "July in Chicago" is used by permission of Phyllis Jackson, Executor, The Estate of Lorri Jackson.

Marael Johnson: "Systems Alert" first appeared in *A.K.A. Magazine* and is used by permission of the author.

Marilyn Johnson: "Our Mothers Were Sisters" from *A Necessary Fire*, published by Event Horizon Press, copyright 1991 by Marilyn Johnson, originally appeared in *Partisan Review*. It is used by permission of the author.

Donald Justice: "A Winter Ode to the Old Men of Lummus Park, Miami, Florida" © 1981 by Donald Justice, is reprinted from *The Summer Anniversaries* (rev. ed.), Wesleyan University Press. By permission of University Press of New England. The 1959 Lamont Poetry Selection.

Susan Kennedy: "Dancing with the Dog" first appeared in *The Tomcat*, Summer, 1990, and is used by permission of the author.

X. J. Kennedy: "On the Proposed Seizure of Twelve Graves in a Colonial Cemetery" and "At the Last Rights for Two Hotrodders," © 1985 by X. J. Kennedy. Reprinted with permission of the author and the publisher, University of Georgia Press.

Rudy Kikel: "Mother," from *Autographs*, 1955, is used by permission of the author.

D. H. Lloyd: "Bible Bob Responds to a Jesus Honker" is used by permission of the author and Applezaba Press (Long Beach).

Gerald Locklin: "california," first published in *Poop* (Mag Press, Long Beach, CA), and "a constituency of dunces," first published in *a constituency of dunces* (Slipstream Press, Niagara Falla, NY) are both reprinted by permission of the author.

Susan Ludvigson: "Love at Cooter's Carpet, Fort Lawn, S.C." is used by permission of the author.

Leo Mailman: "Mrs. Greta Freeport Baxter" is used by permission of the author.

Nichola Manning: "Three Cars" was published by Applezaba Press (Long Beach), and is used by permission of the publisher.

Al Masarik: "Kentucky Woman" and "Boarded Up" are used by permission of the author.

Dan Masterson: "Bloodline" first appeared in *Poetry Miscellany* and then in *World without End*, published by The University of Arkansas Press. © 1991 by Dan Masterson.

Gerald McCarthy: "Note in a Bottle" is used by permission of the author.

Walter McDonald: "The Night of Rattlesnake Chili" was published in *After the Noise of Saigon* by Walter McDonald (University of Massachusetts Press, 1988) and is used by permission of the author.

Jo McDougall: "Edge of America," "Story," and "A Bottomlands Farmer Suffers a Sea Change" appeared in *Towns Facing Railroads*, published by The University of Arkansas Press. © 1991 by Jo McDougall.

Colleen J. McElroy: "With Bill Pickett at the 101 Ranch," © 1987 by Colleen J. McElroy, is reprinted from *Bone Flames* (Wesleyan University Press) by permission of University Press of New England.

Louis McKee: "Salt Peanuts" first appeared in *Pearl* (Number 7, Fall/Winter 1988), Joan Jobe Smith, editor, 3030 E. Second Street, Long Beach, CA 90803. Reprinted in *No Matter* (1987, Pig in the Poke Press, P.O. Box 81925, Pittsburgh, PA 15217). Used by permission of the author.

Peter Meinke: "The Vietnamese Fisherman on Tampa Bay" first appeared in *Delos*, Vol. 1, #2, 1988. Used by permission of the author.

William Meredith: "Rhode Island" is reprinted by permission of the publisher, Alfred A. Knopf, Inc.

Janice Mirikitani: "Jade" was published in *Shedding Silence, Poetry and Prose* by Janice Mirikitani, (Celestial Arts Publishing, Berkeley, CA 1987). © copyright by Janice Mirikitani. Reprinted by permission of the author.

Todd Moore: "after work" is used by permission of the author.

Peter Morris: "The White Sand" is used by permission of the author.

Stanley Moss: "Potato Song" is used by permission of the author.

Eric Nelson: "Everywhere Pregnant Women Appear," first published in *Light Year 88/89*, and "Columbus of the Alphabet" are from *The Interpretation of Waking Life*, published by The University of Arkansas Press. © 1991 by Eric Nelson.

Howard Nemerov: "Landscape with Self-Portrait" and "Found Poem" are reprinted from *War Stories*, published in 1987, by the University of Chicago Press. Copyright 1987 by Howard Nemerov (1929–1991), who was named Poet Laureate of the United States in 1988. The poems are reprinted from it by permission.

Duane Niatum: "Warrior Artists of the Southern Plains: I. Prisoners at Fort Marion: 1875-1878, III. Howling Wolf (1850-1927), Cheyenne" was originally published in *The Michigan Quarterly Review*, © copyright by the author. Used by permission of the author.

Kurt Nimmo: "All the Women in Suburbia" is used by permission of the author.

Kathleen Norris: "Pommes de Terre" first appeared in *Chicago Review* 36:2 (Autumn 1988): 31-32. "At Anfinson's in Hettinger, North Dakota" first appeared in *Plainswoman*, and was published in *The Year of Common Things*, Wayland Press, 1988. Both poems reprinted by permission of the author.

Naomi Shihab Nye: "The Saddest Cowboy in Texas" and "Blood" are used by permission of the author.

Ed Ochester: "Leechburg, PA" is used by permission of the author.

Sharon Olds: "Summer Solstice, New York City" first appeared in *The New Yorker* and was published in *The Gold Cell* (Alfred A. Knopf, 1987). Reprinted by permission of the publisher.

Simon Ortiz: "Canyon de Chelly" is used by permission of the author.

Alicia Ostriker: "The Pure Products of America" is used by permission of the author.

Ron Padgett: "Sonnet" is used by permission of the author.

Greg Pape: "Storm Pattern" is used by permission of the author.

Lizbeth Parker: "A Girl My Age" is used by permission of the author.

Molly Peacock: "Subway Vespers" first appeared in *Verse Magazine,* Vol. 7, No. 3, and is reprinted by permission of the author.

Robert Peters: "Hollywood Boulevard Cemetery" first appeared in *Pearl Magazine* and is reprinted by permission of the author.

Richard Pflum: "Putting It Somewhere" first appeared in *Exquisite Corpse* and is reprinted by permission of the author.

Marge Piercy: "What's That Smell in the Kitchen" from *Circles on the Water* by Marge Piercy. Copyright © 1982 by Marge Piercy. Reprinted by permission of Alfred A. Knopf, Inc., and the Wallace Literary Agency, Inc.

Frank Polite: "In My Black Book" is used by permission of the author.

Ralph Pomeroy: "River's End" © 1991 by Ralph Pomeroy. Printed with the permission of Ralph Pomeroy.

James Purdy: "The Brooklyn Branding Parlors" and "Solitary in Brooklyn" are used by permission of the author.

Karen Randlev: "The Sound of Drums" and "Progress" first appeared in *Exquisite Corpse* and are reprinted by permission of the author.

Brent Reiten: "Sex with Zsa Zsa and Eva Gabor" was published in *Transient Sex* (Scalding Press, P.O. Box 74, Fairfax, CA 94930) and is reprinted by permission of the author.

Carlos Reyes: "Moon Mullins" is used by permission of the author.

Alberto Rios: "Incident at Imuris" and "Singing the Internationale" are used by permission of the author.

Richard Robbins: "The Change to One-Way after Repaving" and "Vandal" are used by permission of the author.

Len Roberts: "Ten Below" is used by permission of the author.

Kirk Robertson: "drawing to an inside straight" and "driving to Vegas" are reprinted from *Driving to Vegas: New & Selected Poems 1969–87* (Sun/Gemini Press).

Vern Rutsala: "Northwest Passage" is used by permission of the author.

Reg Saner: "Where I Come From" is used by permission of the author.

Lynne Savitt: "I'm Glad You Are Casually Interested . . . " first

Belinda Subraman: "El Paso Sex" and "H$_2$O" are used by permission of the author.

William Talcott: "Boogie Board" is used by permission of the author.

Henry Taylor: "Projectile Point, Circa 2500 B.C." is reprinted by permission of Louisiana State University Press from *The Flying Change* by Henry Taylor. Copyright © 1985 by Henry Taylor.

Joanne Townsend: "Something That Has to Do With . . ." is used by permission of the author and Minotaur Press.

Paul Trachtenberg: "Laguna" and "Mystic Craze" are reprinted from *Making Waves* by permission of the author.

David Trinidad: "Driving Back from New Haven" is used by permission of the author.

William Trowbridge: "Late Fall Night" first appeared in *The Kenyon Review* and then in *Enter Dark Stranger*, published by The University of Arkansas Press. © 1989 by William Trowbridge.

Mona Van Duyn: "In the Missouri Ozarks" reprinted with the permission of Atheneum Publishers, an imprint of Macmillan Publishing Company, from *Letters from a Father and Other Poems* by Mona Van Duyn. Copyright © 1982 by Mona Van Duyn.

Mark Vinz: "Roadside Attraction" first appeared in *North Dakota Quarterly*, Vol. 53, No. 3 (Summer 1983) and then in *Mixed Blessings*, Spoon River Poetry Press, copyright © 1989 by Mark Vinz, and is reprinted by permission of the author.

Fred Voss: "Edgy" first appeared in *Poetry/LA*, and is reprinted by permission of the publisher. "The Stud" and "Lingo" first appeared in *The Wormwood Review* and are reprinted by permission of the publisher.

David Wagoner: "My Father's Football Game" is used by permission of the author.

Diane Wakoski: "The Ring of Irony" is reprinted by permission of Black Sparrow Press.

Charles Webb: "Dr. Invisible and Mr. Hide" first appeared in *The Wormwood Review* and is used by permission of the author.

Mark Weber: "Hite Marina, Lake Powell" was first published by Zerx Press and is used by permission of the author.

James Whitehead: "His Slightly Longer Story Song" is used by permission of the author.

Reed Whittemore: "The Destruction of Washington" is used by permission of the author.

INDEX

Rockingham Public Library
540-434-4475
Harrisonburg, Virginia 22801

1. Books may be kept two weeks and may be renewed twice for the same period, unless reserved.

2. A fine is charged for each day a book is not returned according to the above rule. No book will be issued to any person incurring such a fine until it has been paid.

3. All injuries to books beyond reasonable wear and all losses shall be made good to the satisfaction of the Librarian.

4. Each borrower is held responsible for all books charged on his card and for all fines accruing on the same.

GAYLORD